Also by Philip Warner

SIEGES OF THE MIDDLE AGES

THE MEDIEVAL CASTLE

THE HISTORY OF THE SPECIAL AIR SERVICE

THE CRIMEAN WAR: A REAPPRAISAL

BRITISH BATTLEFIELDS: THE SOUTH

BRITISH BATTLEFIELDS: THE NORTH

BRITISH BATTLEFIELDS: THE MIDLANDS

THE JAPANESE ARMY OF THE WORLD WAR II

DISTANT BATTLE

DERVISH: THE RISE AND FALL OF AN AFRICAN EMPIRE

THE SOLDIER

THE SOLDIER

His Daily Life through the Ages

PHILIP WARNER

Taplinger Publishing Company | New York

First published in the United States in 1976 by
TAPLINGER PUBLISHING CO., INC.
New York, New York

Copyright © 1975 by Philip Warner
All rights reserved. Printed in the U.S.A.

Library of Congress Catalog Card Number: 75-10062

ISBN 0-8008-7248-7

‡   ‡   ‡

DRAWINGS, EXCEPT FOR THAT OF THE MONGOL WARRIOR, BORU,
BY JENNY HAWKSLEY

CONTENTS

INTRODUCTION

This is a book about the ordinary soldier. In military history and accounts of battles there is usually much written about the skill of generals and the dash of officers. Subsequently descriptions of campaigns and battles are written by those skilled in literary expression, and with access to records; private soldiers are not usually among such men. There are, of course, soldiers' diaries which have been painstakingly kept, but they are few. In consequence it is easy to forget that ordinary soldiers are the most important part of an army. If there are no soldiers there is no place for officers, however dashing, or for brilliant generals. This fact is well enough appreciated by the generals themselves but tends to be overlooked by historians. *Their* battles are fought by regiments and there are unnamed casualties: in fact a battle is fought by soldier against soldier, and a dead man is a dead man in any language.

Sometimes a present-day soldier will display an amazing aptitude at primitive skills: tracking, hand-to-hand combat, survival, climbing, or weather lore; he himself will be as surprised as anyone to find these deep-down skills, much as a water-diviner or faith-healer may be astonished at his own powers. Soldiers are, of course, more likely than most people to find themselves in circumstances where such skills are necessary and, if a man is lucky, emerge.

Introduction

Some of the soldiers in these pages were lucky and prospered, some were less lucky and were killed; that is the way it is. There is nothing about glory or comradeship or honour in these accounts; they were there of course, but nobody would have thought of mentioning them. Soldiers prefer to talk of more tangible matters like food and women and tobacco and leave.

There can be no one alive today who has not a host of soldiers among his ancestors, although the reader may feel that his own history is quite different from theirs and that his forebears were unlike most of the ruthless, nomadic fighting men in this book. If he thinks that, he should consider the movement of armies (and traders) across the world, and if he finds himself with any unexpected outdoor skills he may take his pick from Vikings, Iberians, Franks, Goths, Vandals, Lombards – and a host of others.

The illustrations in this book, rather than being an attempt to depict the fictional characters in the text, represent ordinary soldiers of each period. Usually historical drawings are stylized, as with the Mongol warrior on page 63 of this book. In all other cases our aim is to show an ordinary, undistinguished soldier. Such men rarely showed by their appearance that they were capable of great endurance and remarkable feats.

THE SOLDIER

VAYLO

The Fighting Man of 3000 BC

Vaylo looked at the food the woman was holding out to him without really seeing it. She had tapped him on the arm as he leaned over the earth parapet straining to see into the mist which still hovered above the plain. He gave a final, searching gaze before turning. She was holding out a flat, dry-looking wheat cake and a jar of mead. He shook his head and turned back to the rampart. It was important to miss nothing; the main body of the enemy might be coming down the centre of the plain but a man could not be sure of it. It might be coming in separate columns or it might have broken up into small parties which were now threading their way through the thickets. You could never tell what the enemy would do particularly the Borae, by all accounts. They would appear in greater or smaller numbers than you expected; they would retreat and seem to be beaten only to have a larger force waiting for you when you left the ramparts and went after plunder. He had fought them twice before and had a fighting man's respect for them. On this autumn morning that respect made him very alert and quick. His throat was slightly dry but he did not want drink at the moment, nor did his stomach want food; it felt curiously light. He was always the same before a fight, wanting it to begin yet half wanting it not to happen. Once it started it was wonderful; he would become very calm and clear-headed.

As he turned back he thought for a moment of the woman. Something in the way she had looked at him printed itself on his mind. She would stay with him. When the fighting began she would be worth two men; she would hand him arrows, throwing stones, axes, even spears; he would never have to look round for weapons. Although there were five men and five women in their group, all sharing everything together, she was – everyone knew – his woman. He had not intended it, it had just happened. All the women were good but she was the best. In the early stages of a battle women could as easily be killed as men; spears and arrows did not distinguish between sexes. Once the armies met hand to hand the women stood back and watched except for passing up a new weapon now and again.

Vaylo

When the battle was over the losers' women were rounded up and made into a work force. The winners' women were in charge and they worked these female slaves harder than ever men would have done. He didn't see his woman putting up with that if it ever came to it. She would either catch the eye of one of the important warriors and become his woman or she would kill her overseer and get herself knocked on the head. She was a strange person; no one knew what she was thinking. An old man had told him that all these dark-haired women had been captured when young girls after a battle with the Silures in which nearly everyone had been killed. The old man did not really trust them but the old were always like that; anything new was dangerous.

Vaylo was not really happy that morning. The news of the Borae advance had come as a surprise. They themselves were still harvesting and were busy with preparations for the winter. Two days ago the tribe had had a bear hunt and killed two. At the end of the day when they had all been pleased with themselves the report had come in that the Borae were on the march. Instead of skinning the bears yesterday and scraping off the fat the whole tribe had been strengthening the earthworks. He cursed the Borae for coming at this time. He himself had just made a new fish trap and it looked like being very successful, but he needed to strengthen it because a big pike had got itself wedged and broken part of it. That would have to wait; these were minor problems. The worst problem was the fact that the Borae were going to catch them defending a very weak position. This was only a cattle fort; these ditches and ramparts were only meant for keeping wild animals away from the flocks at night. If there had been more warning they'd have gone back to their real defensive camp but the Borae might have overtaken them and attacked them on the march. So yesterday had been spent trying to make this structure more defensible. The problem with these cattle forts was that they were too big to be manned by a small force; the only possible plan was to station look-outs on the ramparts at regular intervals and divide the

remainder into three main groups so that one or two could rush
to the point where the main assault was expected. The other
force was kept in reserve for the inevitable surprise attack, on
the flank or perhaps in the rear. Of course if the main thrust
looked like breaking right through then the reserve force would
have to be thrown in there, and the rear and flanks would have
to take their chance.

But Vaylo was no novice; he had fought before and he was
listened to when he spoke in council. He was not a chief,
although if enough people were killed in battle one day he
might be, for the priests seemed to approve of him and if the
priests liked you your chances were very good indeed. The
priests were not thinking of him now; they were too busy praying for the sun to come and dry up the mists which were hiding
the enemy. Perhaps the Borae were praying to their gods to keep
the mists low. Vaylo did not think much of such things; it was
dangerous to think about the gods, they could read your
thoughts and if they were angry there were so many ways they
could hurt you. Vaylo did not mind being killed or wounded in
battle but he dreaded a fever, or being trapped in a swamp, or
being injured and eaten by a wild animal. The gods would do
that to you if you offended them; it was better not to think
about them at all.

Still no movement in the mist. This piece of earthwork he was
standing on was his own special idea. He had asked for it in the
war council yesterday morning. They had listened to him
because of his experience but he could see there were doubters.
He had said that if they were outnumbered – as they were
almost certain to be – they must do something to terrify the
enemy. Men had smiled; the Borae would not easily be terrified.

He explained his plan. The weakest place in the fort was the
main gate where cattle and everything else went in and out.
The Borae were certain to attack there. Well, let them. Instead
of trying to repulse them, let them in. Some of his listeners had
stopped smiling and become angry. Had he gone mad, they
shouted? No, he said. Let them through but build another ram-

4

part behind. As the Borae came through the gate, which would be defended but not very strongly, they would have to turn to the right. This would expose their left sides – until they moved their shields. They would run along this passage thinking they were getting into the inside of the fort. After thirty paces it would turn sharp left again and open out into a square entirely surrounded by ramparts. On them, old men, women, boys, girls, everyone who would not be in the forefront of the battle would be lying ready to leap up and hurl darts and spears on to them. Half their force could be trapped in this way for the real fighters could jump down behind them and force them farther in. There was a murmur of approval. What a slaughter it could be! And the plunder! But he had not quite finished. 'We shall not need all our men for that', he said. 'Let the others slip out quietly and take the rest of the Borae in the rear. As soon as the rest of their army sees the first half go through the ramparts they will think they have won the fort. They too will rush forward and they will be thunderstruck when we attack from behind. They will think it is treachery from their own kind. We'll shout treachery and help them to believe it.'

Well, there it was. All yesterday they had looked at the inner rampart. It was not nearly as good as it should be but it was probably good enough. Unfortunately what with the bear hunt the day before, and the toil all day yesterday, they were now all tired. It was not good to begin a battle feeling tired. However, it had been done and now they were waiting. The Borae always attacked at dawn; why were they not already here?

Suddenly his eye caught a movement. Others had seen it too, and on the ramparts there was a quick flurry of movement. Then all was calm again as men waited and watched.

The Borae were coming up the centre of the plain. There was still too much mist about to see the full extent of their force but the ones who were now in sight were coming forward swiftly and easily. They looked large too. He'd fought Borae before but they had not been as large as this. The root of his tongue suddenly felt stiff and dry but the feeling quickly passed. They were coming straight for the main gate. Good. It would have been disastrous if they had suddenly split the column and encircled the fort. Worse still if they had by-passed the fort altogether and gone marching into the tribal land behind. Fortunately the Borae liked a fight and did not usually bother with tactics. Now they were halting just out of arrow range and were obviously waiting for the whole force to collect. There were a lot of them, 300 perhaps, and every man would be a trained, fit warrior. He almost wished he were one of them. In this tribe you fought when you had to, when you were attacked or if you were short of food and goods. These Borae did nothing but fight, it seemed. It would be interesting, but on the whole he felt he was better being half a soldier and half a hunter.

A chief was now out in front talking to them. Doubtless he was promising them plunder and women and food. It was always the same. Now he was pointing towards the camp and explaining how it should be attacked. He seemed to be explaining a clever plan and Vaylo did not want to be attacked with clever plans, he wanted the Borae to make a stupid rush and all get killed. Their chief was out of arrow or spear range. Vaylo felt uneasy and he knew something must be done. What could reach him and stop him talking? A throwing-stone perhaps. He had several which he had selected and shaped himself. They were flat oval flints, a little larger than his outspread hand. Flung into the air they seemed to ride upwards with the wind and carried a long way. Usually they were hurled into packed troops where they could not miss but they could be aimed precisely; he had once killed a wolf with one, but not at this range. The Borae chief was now walking up and down. It seemed hopeless but Vaylo would try. He slid his fingers over the stone, bent down a little, pivoted in a complete circle and launched the disc-shaped stone. The force of his throw nearly took him off the rampart but he recovered to watch the stone spinning through the air. The Borae chief had walked down the line but suddenly swung round and came back. Fascinated, Vaylo observed that, quite unaware of it, he was coming

towards the path of the stone. *He walked right into it*. As he
turned to say something, pointing at the rampart, the stone
smashed right into his face. The features simply disintegrated
into a mass of blood and bone. He flung up his hands and
staggered, then fell. Enraged, his warriors surged forward.
Whatever he had just been telling them was clearly forgotten.
They moved as a body towards the main gate.

Vaylo was pleased at this but a little quiver ran down his
spine just the same. There seemed to be a lot of Borae and the
speed at which they were coming showed clearly that even with
the help of the trap they would take some defeating. As they
came into range a shower of arrows and slung stones met them.
A few men fell and a few more staggered away out of the charge:
the rest came on but more had probably been wounded and did
not know it. Well, they would soon find out. A flint arrow
could slice half a man's arm off without his realizing in the
excitement of the moment; it felt a glancing harmless blow but
the effects would soon tell. He had seen some terrible wounds
made by flint arrows. Some arrows had a series of flints along
the shaft, set slightly backwards. The man who was hit by one
would be in agony. Vaylo did not care for the trick himself – but
it was typical of the bowmen. He used a bow himself for hunting
but the men who used bows in battle were better than he was.
They were a group apart, though, who did not mix with the rest
of the tribe. Men seemed slightly afraid of the bowmen, as they
were of the priests. Still they were doing great work at the
moment.

By now stones and arrows were beginning to rattle over the
ramparts. A section of the Borae had dropped behind and were
lobbing over the heads of the leading warriors. There were
screams around and behind him. He hoped the women had not
been hit but he did not look round. He was looking for the next
leader. Someone must surely take the place of the one whose face
he had smashed in. They were at the gate now and making a
tremendous charge as they reached it. They had no fear at all,
these Borae! Our own men were now beginning to fall off the

7

ramparts and the Borae were obviously killing too many too quickly. He himself was to the left of the gate at the corner and the chief was on the right. If he'd been chief he'd have been nearer the gate; you could not see enough of what was going on from the corner. The gate was not meant to last long but it was not meant to go as quickly as this. The men behind it were as good as dead. Everyone but themselves had realized when they had been stationed there. They had been told to hold the gate till it broke then jump up on to the ramparts. They had no hope of that, of course; the Borae would be among them and stabbing them to death; they were already at it. This was the central part of the battle but he dared not look; he must still watch in front. The time was not yet ripe for him to get into the fight but it was uncomfortable waiting and thinking. There were plenty of Borae left outside and they were ranging their spears and stones accurately on to the ramparts. There was a lot of screaming going on behind and he hoped that the massacre party which was meant to finish off the trapped Borae was not being driven from its post. If it were it would be a disaster. The Borae would help each other on to the ramparts and all would be lost. Perhaps they should have had more experienced warriors in that sector. There was nothing to be done now, though.

In front he suddenly saw a sight which made his heart sink. Another party, as large as the first, was now advancing out of the mists. The holders of the fort were hopelessly outnumbered, but no battle is lost or won till it is over. There was a chance, although a slim one, that the second detachment of Borae might be defeated by bluff. It would not be easy. His own small force had been held in reserve for a flank attack but with the numbers now showing themselves this could make no difference. If, however, he could get the chief to follow his plan his new scheme might work. Time was vital but he did not dare leave his own position in case some fresh crisis suddenly occurred. He half-turned, without taking his eyes off the scene in front, and spoke to the woman. She was there and she answered as if nothing unusual was happening. As he spoke a stone twanged so close to

8

his head that it seemed to scrape along the skin. 'Go to the chief', he said, 'and tell him I am going to attack the second detachment. Ask him very carefully if he can spare men to join in. Be careful what you say because if we win and he thinks I was giving him orders he will kill me afterwards. Be very careful.'

Death in battle was nothing; it happened without a man knowing, but to be put to death by the chief for trying to take his authority would be very different. He had seen that happen to others and he did not want it to happen to him.

She was gone. He did not know how she would move along the rampart, get past the gap where the gate had been, which would be full of bodies and perhaps still have men fighting, and up the other side. But he knew she would do it. Could she do it quickly enough though?

Behind, there seemed to be less clamour. He longed to go back and look; he should have sent the woman to find out earlier how it was going. He dared not take his eyes off the scene in front. He hurled a few throwing axes at the Borae who had stayed behind when the first party charged through the gatehouse. He wondered what they thought they were doing. They should have followed the others soon after the vanguard had burst through the gate. It was fortunate that they had not. Probably they had been told the first part of the plan by the leader he had wounded, which was to cover the attack, and now they did not know what to do. Well, they would get no more instructions from that leader today, if ever. They were stupid to stay there in the open aiming stones and arrows at defenders they could hardly see. In time they would all be killed, or would have been but for the second detachment coming up behind.

Suddenly the woman was back. He shot a very quick glance at her. She was excited and kept baring her teeth as she spoke. 'The chief is dead', she told him panting. 'They did not know what to do. He was hit by an arrow. I told them that you were now the chief and when you jumped off the ramparts they must follow and attack the Borae from the other flank.'

It was a dangerous thing she had done but he had no time to think of that. At least she had been quick, whereas she might have wasted a lot of time trying to persuade the chief if he had still been alive. He forgot her. He shouted to the other men on the rampart. 'Come', he said. 'Come!'

Down in front there was too much thicket to see much. He ran blindly forward in the direction of where he had seen the Borae second detachment. On the rampart he had been able to see them; now he was lost. But he crashed on. It would at least give them the advantage of surprise.

Suddenly he saw a Borae in front of him. The man was unprepared and completely taken by surprise. He slashed at him with his axe and saw it bite into the man's head. They had only a skin cap on their heads, these Borae, and the sharp axe went right through it. He held the handle and as the man fell, jerked it out of the wound not a second too soon. There were Borae all around him. One aimed a dart at his face; he ducked, swung round and chopped the man on his arm with his axe. As he did so a blow fell on his own shoulder. The pain of it made him lose his grip of the axe handle. He had no weapon, but suddenly although there was fighting all around him he was not being attacked and another axe was thrust into his hand. He just had time to see where it had come from. It was the woman. She must have followed him through the thicket. He had no time to look at her, for a huge Borae with a great stone dagger was suddenly in front of him slashing at his chest. He caught the first blow on his shield but as he twisted with the force of the giant blow the man swung round and aimed a spear he had been holding in the other hand. It missed, and as the man launched it he fell forward. Like a flash he swung the axe the woman had brought him into the Borae's neck. A great spurt of blood shot out and over him. The Borae was down; there were others, but they were tiring. He saw the back of another and sank his axe into it. Again he lost the axe as the man fell; again the woman was there. But now the fight had changed; they were no longer being attacked. He saw a Borae, but he was no warrior, he was trying to flee. He let him go. He was a follower, a bearer of burdens, and as he fled in panic he would cause others to flee. At this moment he felt a sharp, bitter pain in his shoulder. He turned in dismay. It was an arrow, deep in the flesh. For a moment he staggered, and the scene swirled around him. Then he recovered. He could not use his left arm but now there was no need. The battle was won here. If it was also won in the fort all was well.

The woman was now holding his arm and trying to take out the arrow. It came. It had not hooked itself into a bone and it came out with a stream of blood. From somewhere she produced a wad of spider's web, and put it in the hole. The blood turned dark but ceased to well up so fast; then it stopped.

Feeling slightly numbed and bewildered he looked around. There were more Borae dead than he had realized; surprise must have had a greater effect than he had expected. He turned a body over with his foot; it was dangerous to touch the dead for they had become immortal and could hurt you; it seemed better to push with the foot as you might do if you had stumbled by accident. The body had a long, narrow face and very fair hair, different from their own round faces and brown hair, different again from the woman, who was small but very lithe and active. Around this man's neck was a circle of coloured stones. He must have been a chief, for only chiefs wore such necklaces. He was probably a very important man for he was with the second party, therefore a proved warrior who no longer had to justify himself in the front assault. Suddenly he realized with a shock that the woman had come past him and was pulling off the necklace. She must have gone mad in the fight for she straightened up and slipped it over his own head. He was annoyed and was putting up his hand to pull it off when a man came bounding into the clearing, waving an axe. It was one of their own men. 'We have won,' he shouted. 'They are killing the last of them in the fort. Come and see.'

Vaylo turned and with the woman still close by him walked briskly back to the fort. It was true. There were dead Borae everywhere. Shouting and yelling, the men came out of the fort, some of them with wounds and all wild with excitement. Among them he noticed Lar, who might now be chief. Lar was calling a council. Clearly he wished to make it obvious at this moment that he *was* the new chief. It was not absolutely certain that he would be chosen because it must be approved by the tribe and Lar was not a great warrior; even now he had little blood on him and he did not seem to be wounded.

Lar spoke. 'The chief is dead,' he said. 'He wished me to be chief if he were killed. I am now chief.' There was a little murmur from the assembled tribe. Lar looked at Vaylo who had said nothing, for he did not care who was chief. 'What is that necklace?' he said. 'Where did you get it?'

'It was on one of the Borae,' said Vaylo.

'Give it me,' said Lar. 'It is a chief's necklace.'

At his side he heard a hiss. It was the woman.

'Do not give it him,' she said.

Lar heard and turned to her. 'This woman', he said suddenly in a clear, high voice, 'on the rampart I saw her. She killed the chief. She came up behind him in the battle and cut his head with an axe. Kill her, kill them both.' He turned to the tribe, who stood watching silently.

Suddenly everything had become very still. Only one thing moved. It was the woman. She moved quickly but quietly to Vaylo's side and pushed an axe into his hand. He took it, looked at her, looked round the circle, then suddenly with a violent movement smashed it right through Lar's face. There was a sound like a long sigh from the tribe but nobody moved.

'Yes,' he said, putting his foot on Lar's body. 'I am the chief and this is my woman. We have beaten the Borae. We are the greatest tribe on the earth. Drag away the bodies for the wolves to eat, repair the defences and then we will feast. We are the conquerors of the Borae, and I am your chief and this is my woman. Go! Move quickly for there may be more of them.'

He turned and looked at her, expecting to see her smiling.

But she was looking past him at Garo – one of the warriors.
Garo was looking sulky.

'There will be trouble there,' she said.

'I will watch it,' he answered.

She smiled faintly. 'I too,' she said. 'Am I not your woman?'

The year was 3000 BC. Vaylo was a successful chief and under
his rule the tribe extended their fields. The outlines of those
fields still remain, for they carried the stones to the sides and
thus marked out a pattern. They grew wheat and barley with a
poor yield. They were clever with their flint axes and cut down
trees to build huts. They buried their dead in long tombs called
'barrows'.

Vaylo's graves and forts (which we would call 'causeway
camps') were not large and were destroyed first by weather and
then by ploughing. But though most of the visible relics of his
tribe were destroyed and even the tribe itself became merged
with others, the children of Vaylo and his woman remained
distinctive. Many other invaders came and fought over his fort.
Some built stone tombs, all had different religions and all
brought a new skill or weapon which enabled them to win wars.
Some came with bronze, others with iron. By the year 100 BC it
seemed as if civilization had reached a stage it would never
surpass. The new invaders were the Belgae, a people from
northern France. They had kings and coinage, metalwork,
leather and slaves. One of them married a girl he found in a
village near the Kennet. The girl was different from the others
he had met. Wherever he went she seemed to be close by; she
even seemed to know what he was thinking.

VARRUS

The Roman Legionary

Varrus was in trouble – again. He had been late for the morning training parade – in fact the sun was well up into the sky before he woke up – and, of course, the centurion, Liga, was drilling his men when he arrived. Liga hated him and, by Jupiter, it was mutual. That suited Varrus; he liked people to know his feelings but the difficulty was that Liga was a centurion, and Varrus only commanded a *contubernium*.*

It gave Liga great pleasure to find everything wrong with Varrus's contubernium. They were perfect, of course, Varrus knew that. They would do anything for him and when Liga had discovered he was not on parade at dawn they would have had some excuse for him. Liga would know they were lying and set out to make them pay for it. It was very easy for Liga; everything the men did would be wrong; their swords would be dull and blunt, their clothing slack and their training-drill, that would be the worst he had ever seen. Varrus bared his teeth as he thought of it. Liga, a creeping half-wit who owed his position entirely to the fact that his uncle was a senator. All the other centurions had worked their way up through the ranks and knew the job backwards with their eyes shut. Not Liga though; Liga was carried by the other centurion, Marcus, and the fact that the legion had fought from Numidia to Caledonia. Not a man in it was Roman by birth although they had all acquired Roman citizenship by service. Liga was Roman of course. That flabby, puffy look, that vindictive pettiness couldn't be anything else. Now perhaps he was being a little unfair; Corus, his first centurion had been Roman born and he had been as straight as a die and as brave a man as you'd wish to serve under.

All these thoughts ran through Varrus's head as he stood there waiting for Liga to finish making fools of the contubernium. Liga had seen him, of course, and just carried on, knowing full well that to give the men hell in front of their decanus – and because of his fault – was the very best thing he could do

*Basically a contubernium was an eight man group. On frontier posts it became a ten man group commanded by a decanus.

if he happened to be that sort of bastard, which he was. Suddenly he decided to see Varrus and with elaborate courtesy said, 'Ah, good morning, Varrus. You have been delayed I see. I hope you are not ill. Take your command and come and see me after training. They are not very good. We must have a talk about them. We may be able to stiffen them with some good men from other contubernia.'

Not very good! Varrus turned to stone. Not very good! These men, he thought, were great fighting soldiers when you were a snivelling baby crawling round the floor getting your first experience of licking up spittle. But all he said was, 'Liga', in a sharp tone as a good soldier does whatever the insult or the provocation because you don't win wars by fighting within your own army. He knew how to deal with Liga – years of experience in the army had taught him that. It was to wait and remember. There might be a time, a chance, but it was not now. You might as well shout back at thunder as try to argue with the centurion.

The contubernium looked at him. They didn't mind that Liga had given them a rough time and they bore no resentment against Varrus for it. They knew what had happened to Varrus and they knew that if they'd been late on parade or were late in the future Varrus would show no mercy. That was the system, that was why the Roman army always won.

Varrus did not want their sympathy and he gave them a rougher handling than usual to show it. There was no room for softness in the Roman army; it was bigger than all of them. He'd been a fool to chase that girl and drink so much wine and be late; he'd made mistakes before, but this was a bad one. He was not feeling too good after all that wine and it was getting hot. It went on for four hours this parade but it seemed like four years. At last the 'Stand down' was sounded. Varrus was starving and quickly made his way to the mess tent. Hardly had he filled his plate with pulse soup when a messenger stood before him. 'Liga wants to see you,' said the creature, and disappeared.

Varrus looked at the plate of peas and beans in front of him, warm, satisfying, just what he wanted. Four hours of drill – well three and a half, nothing to eat at dawn (but that had been his own fault) and now this call from Liga. Well, you didn't disobey a centurion. Varrus put down his plate and walked briskly off.

Liga was not in his tent when Varrus arrived. He did not appear for half an hour. When he arrived he made a gesture of surprise. 'You are early,' he said. 'I told the messenger I wanted to see you after the meal. You must have eaten very quickly.' Varrus looked at him stonily. Liga clearly expected him to say something but Varrus said nothing. He had no intention of letting Liga know that he had now missed two meals this day and his stomach was like an empty bag. Liga was irritated by this blunt refusal to respond to what he thought had been a friendly gesture. He had, in fact, no intention of diminishing his plans for the rest of Varrus's day but he liked to think that his subordinates appreciated his interest in their welfare. Varrus knew perfectly well that the sort of loose, imprecise order which Liga had given to the messenger was always misinterpreted and he despised Liga for it.

'Varrus', said the centurion, 'your contubernium looked lethargic and casual to me this morning. As we both know, they are old soldiers and they have developed a way of doing everything with the minimum effort. Their sword practice was a waste of time, for they put no effort into it. You have seen them so often that you probably do not notice that they are making no effort at all, although, of course, they do not make any mistakes either. They need sharpening up.'

Varrus looked at him steadily but did not speak. It was partly true, but he would back them against any other contubernium in the Roman army none the less.

Liga continued: 'Sharpening up is what they require and sharpening up is what they shall have. We are holding this line to keep the barbarians in their place before we subdue them. I need not tell you the Roman army always wins, nor do I need to tell you how and why it does so.'

No you don't, do you, thought Varrus, considering that I was helping to make conquests when you were still whining around as a schoolboy. But he said nothing.

'Soon', said Liga, 'we shall press forward again, marching, fortifying our camps and beating any opposition. Today you will rehearse the first move. You will take out your contubernium, march ten miles, mark out a camp, dig the outer trench and wait for me. I shall come out and inspect it.'

Varrus stared at him in amazement. The man was mad. Everybody knew that since their great defeat six years before at Mons Graupius the Caledonians had been planning their revenge. This line the legion was holding was a mere token. You cannot spread 6,000 men over seventy miles and convince anyone it is a defence. When he had fought with the great Agricola six years earlier the Romans had won, but no one in the field on that day had gone away with the idea that the Caledonians were a defeated army. This line they were picketing between the Solway and the Tyne was a sort of truce border. If the Caledonians drove through it the Romans would close up and cut off their retreat and the enemy knew that; they were not stupid and they would only try it if they had secretly amassed huge numbers and could spring a surprise. By the same token, if the Romans probed forward the Caledonians would lead them on, then suddenly turn and massacre them. And this lunatic Liga was proposing that as a training exercise his contubernium should go forward, choose a position they had not the men to defend, and then come back through the lines the Caledonians would certainly have put around them. Liga would never reach them, if he was mad enough to try. By the time he came out the enemy would be tired of the game and would chop him and his escort into little pieces. Well that would be one good thing. But their own position was a delightful one: *they must stay there* till he arrived. Well that would be never. There was no chance of their being able to slip back under cover of darkness because Liga might well have decided to leave them there all night. If therefore they arrived back before he had even set out, it was execution for Varrus and flogging for the contubernium. Either way, stay or go, the contubernium was doomed. He looked at Liga with a half smile on his face. 'What a very good idea,' he said.

It was a long speech for Varrus and Liga was slightly taken aback. For a moment he warmed to the decanus. 'Good', he said. 'Do this well and I will speak well of you to the tribune. Then, when the next vacancy for a centurion occurs he will probably appoint you.'

Varrus listened impassively. I would rather be a *miles*, a common soldier of the lowest rank, than be promoted by your favour, he thought. Liga thought the decanus was too over-whelmed with gratitude to be able to speak. He felt encouraged and went on. 'You bear a great name, Varrus. At the beginning of this century the commander of the Roman army in Germany was Publius Quinctilius Varus. He could have been your ancestor. Unfortunately he was killed in an ambush in which three legions were destroyed. It is said that some of the Germans in the legions changed sides again in the battle. But he was a great Roman general.'

I bet he was, thought Varrus. It's amazing how they always find an excuse for their defeats particularly when they're due to their own stupidity. But rather to his surprise he found himself speaking. 'I am not Roman. I am of the Belgae people who were in southern England when the Roman armies first came here. I am only a Roman citizen because I am a soldier in the Roman army. I know nothing of Publius Quinctilius Varus.' He sneered slightly as he mouthed the name.

Liga did not miss the undertone. He took a step towards the decanus and glared at him. He was slightly taller than Varrus but as he stood there he had an uneasy feeling that Varrus was running a critical eye over him, inspecting him in fact. The decanus was fully dressed and armed. His tunic was tightly looped to give his bare legs full freedom of movement. Over his woollen tunic his *lorica*, a corselet of strip metal, fitted closely, his dagger on one side and sword on the other looked rightly placed for instant use, and, giving him extra height, was the great, plumed, bronze helmet. He looked as if he could march twenty-four miles and fight a battle without turning a hair. In fact he was hot, hungry, and tired but he could do all and more than could be asked of him. Confronting Varrus, Liga, dressed only in tunic and sandals and carrying only a personal dagger, felt irritatingly inferior. 'Very well', he said with a wave of dismissal, 'you have your instructions. The men will have eaten. Take them off straight away.'

Varrus swung round on his heel and walked back to the billet. Six men were asleep on their beds – clearly carrying out the old soldier's precept: never stand when you can sit, never sit when you can lie down – two were gambling, and two were lounging in the doorway. It would be the same all over the camp. In every group there were always the sleepers, the gamblers, the unofficial look-outs, a comedian, a bellyacher, a boaster, a man with a problem . . .

'Turn out!' he yelled. Within seconds they were there. Two, he could have sworn, were still asleep but they were standing upright before him, weapons loose, ready to move.

'We are going', he said in firm, crisp tones, 'to march out ten miles, dig the outline trenches of a *castra exploratorum*, hold off any attacks until Liga, the centurion, arrives, and then if he passes our workmanship we shall return to camp.' He paused and watched his words sink into their minds. 'We shall take three extra javelins each', he continued, 'a day's rations, and the tent. We may have to stay there till tomorrow.'

'Or for ever,' someone muttered. Varrus did not hear it; this was no time for bothering about petty indiscipline; the man might be dead tomorrow as they all might.

'Any problems?' he asked.

Pero raised his hand. 'I know that orders are orders,' he said. 'But does the centurion know that the sentries report large numbers of Picts ahead of our line and are expecting an attack any day?'

Varrus ignored the question. Pero is even more stupid than

he looks, he thought. However he noted that the man had called the enemy the *Picti*, that is, the painted ones. The Romans painted themselves too sometimes, partly for camouflage and partly to inspire fear. Plenty of armies did it. But these Caledonians as he called them, although the tribunes said the tribe opposite were Selgovae, used more paint than most and often wore nothing else. If they were heavily painted, this probably meant imminent attack.

'Right,' he said. 'Fall out and be back here ready to march in ten minutes.'

They fell out. One paused for a second. 'That woman you were with yesterday, she was looking for you when you were seeing Liga. She said she wanted to give you something but the picket chased her out of the camp lines.'

Varrus nodded. He realized she was probably a spy. Well, that was the end of it; these local women around frontier posts were likely to be very dangerous.

As the contubernium paraded they attracted a certain amount of curiosity. For one thing they were very heavily loaded. The *dolabrae* (pick-axes) were a burden as were the measuring instruments, the tent, the extra javelins, making each man's total five, the semi-circular long shields, spare thongs, a cloak, personal kit for washing and shaving, and rations. They, were as strong as horses, they had been trained by using ultra-heavy weapons and by practising with the *onagers* (giant catapults used in sieges) which could be handled only by strong men, but the assignment now in front of them was more than enough. A legionary could march twenty-four miles in twenty-four hours over a fair surface, but their present task was to march ten miles over very rough ground, dig trenches and probably fight as well. Secretly, he doubted if they would live to tell the tale.

As they set out into the unknown, the sentries ironically waved them goodbye. The contubernium made good time at first. Pero was counting the paces (Liga would of course check it later) and the first four miles went easily; the country was open and there was no sign of the enemy. Varrus did not doubt that they were there but they were keeping well out of sight. At the end of the hour they halted. Men adjusted their thongs, rearranged their burdens, and looked around. Halts were short, for they destroyed the rhythm of the march if they were too long. Suddenly someone said: 'There's a Pict behind us.' They all stared. 'No it's not,' someone else said. 'It's a woman – a follower, she's trying to catch up.'

It was indeed a woman. As she came closer Varrus had a second shock. Not only was it a woman, it was his woman, the woman who had made him late and caused all this trouble. For a moment he felt an urge to chop her with his sword. She hurried up and held out her closed hand to him. 'You left this last night,' she said and unclenched her fingers: it was his ring.

She looked very frightened and as she stood there she glanced anxiously into the hills ahead. The contubernium looked at her scowling. She's a spy, they thought. Being a woman, she has now betrayed her own people because of a man. She hopes they have not seen her but she's certain to be wrong.

'Go back,' said Varrus. He turned to the men. 'March on,' he ordered. He glanced back once. She was still standing there.

By the time they had covered ten miles they were very hot and weary. The going had been very rough, sometimes hilly, sometimes loose stones, sometimes treacherous swamp. They had not been attacked so far but they had seen plenty of movement around them. The enemy were clearly surprised at this unusual move but they would soon recover and come in to the kill. However, until that happened there was work to do.

Varrus chose a site with the best observation he could find. It was not good; there was too much scrub and a ridge on one side meant that the enemy could approach to fifty paces unseen, but it was on a hillock and the ground could be dug. He had often seen men choose ideal camp sites only to find the rock was so close to the soil you could not dig a ditch. Here the soil was sandy and could soon be moved. This, being a temporary battle camp, was half the usual size and measured 100 metres by 50. It was almost a perfect rectangle but the ground fell away on

the south-west corner so the outline was indented at that point
to make full use of the high ground. One road ran directly
north-south and the other, which crossed it in the centre of the
camp, ran east-west. The gateway openings for the north-south
road were slightly wider than the others. This was merely a
matter of marking lines and putting down flags. The outer ditch
had to be completed, which meant digging all round the perimeter to a depth of one metre; it was also a metre wide. The
soil from it was thrown up on the outer side, making a parapet.
It was hard work, but Varrus did not put everyone on it; he
detailed one man as sentry and took the north and east himself
while the sentry looked to the west and south. At intervals he
changed the sentry and even took a turn with the digging himself; the fact that he had had no food so far that day made him
feel unusually tired and rather light-headed. His turn on the
digging was not to make the men feel that leader and men were
one unit – they knew that already – but to lighten their task a
little while finding out for himself what the soil felt like. They
did not expect him to dig but they muttered about having the
other sentry, which seemed a waste of digging power.

The enemy had noticed them all right. Varrus could see men
moving on the hills, converging towards them. When they
reached the lower ground they were no longer visible. He
guessed they were puzzled and cautious. Possibly they suspected
a trap, that this small detachment was a lure to bring them out
into the open. They would not be likely to believe that this was
an isolated unit but would think that there must be dozens like
it and that soon several thousand men would follow. Long may
they continue to think so, he said to himself, because once they
realize the true position we are dead, and painfully dead too.

When the perimeter ditch was almost completed he took
three men off the party and set them to collect large stones.
With these he began to build a *sangar*, an enclosure of stones in
the middle of the camp where the *principia*, the headquarters
building, would eventually be. This was a slow business for
what seems a large number of stones when you are finding and

carrying them becomes a very small quantity when you are trying to build four walls into a seven-metre square. But eventually that was done, not well or even adequately, but the best that could be done in the time and circumstances. This was a desperate attempt at self-preservation and was not part of his official task. Strictly speaking he should have continued to mark out spaces for barracks and store rooms and baths and so on but he decided that immediate military necessities took precedence. The next military priority was food and a short rest. The contubernium had been on the move, one way and another, since dawn, apart from the midday meal which he himself had missed. Tired, hungry men do not see so clearly, fight so fiercely, or last so well. He ordered them to rest while the meal was prepared, and rest again after it. It was now evening and Liga was unlikely to come for he could not return while the light lasted; clearly he was planning to come the next day. Varrus swept the surrounding countryside with his discerning eye; there was no further movement in the hills. He gave orders for the night. One by one the soldiers went to the near-by stream, drank, washed their feet, and filled their containers with water. He detailed the sentries. Everything was quiet. As they waited for night to fall Varrus felt a curious prickling sensation at the back of his neck. He knew he was being observed by unseen watchers and felt as if he were on a stage surrounded by darkness. It all seemed curiously unreal. He looked at the soldiers; each had found his pitch for the night inside the *sangar* and shaped the earth to his liking. If they thought they were doomed they did not show it. He looked as aloof and nonchalant as he always did and this, perhaps, gave them confidence, however falsely based.

The attack came soon after dark. A shout from the north sentry brought them to their feet. Each soldier was holding his javelin and as the enemy came to the *sangar* he stabbed sharply at the dark, glistening, squirming forms ahead. The enemy needed to close to use their short swords. In the dark they looked like demons and when the javelins went in they gave wild, unearthly screams which would have been terrifying at any other time. He himself stood in the middle of the *sangar* waiting for the inevitable moment when one broke through and came in. Within minutes Pero – big-mouthed Pero – had been stabbed by one man as his javelin stuck in another, and a man was through. Varrus swung lightly towards him and drove his sword into the man's throat. He snatched it out as the man fell but there was another coming at him on his left. He flung up his shield and battered him back but the *sangar* was now full of people, struggling, stabbing, confused. He saw one Pict stab another by mistake but now he had backed into the corner and was holding off two. Then he felt a dull blow on his shoulder near his neck and found himself falling forward. His shield fell and he tried to bring up his left arm to ward off another blow but it would not move. Then the darkness became complete.

The victors went on fighting in the *sangar* for a while after all the Romans were dead. In the dark, without a commander, they could not see what had happened and perhaps with their war frenzy roused they could not stop stabbing and hacking. Then they stopped, but soon began to fight again over the spoil. Varrus was buried under no less than five mutilated, naked bodies and in the dark his body was not seen. Still quarrelling, the victorious Selgovae left the *sangar*.

Varrus's long day had come to an end. What had begun with a drunken hangover had finally ended with four stab wounds, one in the neck, one in the thigh, one in the back and one in the right arm. He had also had a blow with a club on the head. Had he known what was happening he would have considered it a very worthy end for a Roman warrior.

At dawn the woman crept cautiously up to the *sangar*. The sight of the twisted bodies, the congealed blood and the gaping wounds did not deter her. She glanced towards the hills anxiously, but saw no one. Then one by one she turned over the corpses until she found Varrus. She looked at him and with a half-smile noted his wounds. Then she leant forward and pressed her lips gently on to his.

Suddenly she shot upright. Varrus's lips were warm. She bent down again and listened. He was breathing faintly. Like a dart she dashed to the stream. Gradually she moistened his lips and washed his face; she did not touch his wounds which were still oozing a little blood, then she watched, waiting for him to recover consciousness.

This was how Liga found them. He came out with an escort of two contubernia and did not see a single Pict on the way. They saw him but they thought he would camp and they would kill him and his men that night, just as they had dealt with Varrus's men the day before. But Liga's men did not stay. They buried the Romans in the *sangar* after first flinging the Pict bodies outside for the wolves and wild cats to eat. Varrus was put on a litter and taken back to camp; the woman was allowed to nurse him but he could never fight again. Liga was reprimanded by the cohort commander for having wasted valuable Roman lives when manpower was so short. He was sent to Deva (Chester) to the Second Legion. Soon afterwards the Second Legion was sent to the Suebo-Sarmatic War where Liga was killed, and that was the end of his tantrums and his politico-military ambitions.

Varrus took many months to recover but then because of his wounds and his military record was made a local camp commandant. Ten years later the Romans decided to build a permanent wall from the Solway to the Tyne and Varrus supervised some of the construction camps. He had, of course, settled down with the woman and they had four restless sons. The eldest left home and went to Eboracum (York) with the legion and raised a family there. Seven hundred years later the family were still there long after the Roman occupation of Britain had been forgotten, and in spite of the wars in which they had taken part.

ROLF
The Viking

Rolf was land-hungry. He had nothing but his father's sword. He had never known his father; before he went on his first voyage, when he was fifteen, his mother had told him a strange story but he was not very curious because it did not seem to matter what a man's parents were or where they had come from. What mattered was the ship and the sea and the storms and the fight; and after that the drinking. He could not see how it could matter who your mother and father were.

His mother was very beautiful, even now. She had had nine children, and three of them were by Eric with whom she now lived. She had told him that his father, who she said was named Leif, and whom he could not remember, had captured her in a raid on England and brought her back to Norway. The Vikings had killed her husband in England but she was already pregnant and when she arrived back in Halden she bore a son. Leif was pleased that she bore men children and named him Rolf. His mother bore two more sons to Leif and then he did not return from one of his many voyages.

When it was clear he would never come back his mother took another man. There was no marriage in Halden but some people swore to stay together and whatever happened, all children were equal in rights. Thus Rolf had Leif's sword although he was not really Leif's son, and the sword was a man's most treasured possession. Each warrior had a very valuable sword, heavily decorated with gold, which he left at home and when he went away he took less ornamental weapons. At one time Rolf had eight half-brothers but, by the time he was twenty, six had already been killed or lost on voyages. Of the two left, one was an adventurer like himself but the other was a *niddering*, a nothing who did not like the sea and said he would stay at home and help his parents until his father died and he could inherit the piece of poor land the family owned. There were plenty of fish in the Tista river but the land was too rocky and steep to grow good crops. Halden was a convenient place to live if you were a fighting man and an adventurer. Centuries later it would become part of the border between Norway and

Sweden; a great castle would be built here and the mighty Charles XII of Sweden would be killed attacking it. But that was all nearly a thousand years in the future. In the early ninth century the banks of the Tista had few advantages. There were too many people and there was too little land up here, so the land that a family farmed gave a poor living unless you brought back plunder from overseas.

All these thoughts ran through Rolf's mind as the boat drove through the seas. It smashed and leapt its way along, carrying every inch of sail it could take, and bucked and rolled like a wild horse. Rolf was the steersman. They took this job in turns, for holding the great steering oar was a task which soon tired the strongest. This crew was known as 'the Madmen' for they were wild and reckless even by Viking standards. In a storm they made no effort to shorten sail but allowed the wind to hustle them along as fast as it could. One day they would come to a rocky coast, perhaps, and be smashed to pieces before they could turn; but that was another day.

At this moment dawn was just breaking and the ship was bounding south in weather which he loved. The sea was rough but not so rough that they were thrown around like a piece of driftwood and blown off course, nor was it so calm that they had to take out the oars and row to help it along. With this wind they could cover 200 miles in a day, although it was not necessary to do so on this day. Already Rolf could smell the land; it was strange that when you were on land you could smell the sea but when you were at sea you could tell you were approaching land from as far as fifty miles away; it was a dank, earthy smell, quite unmistakable.

It was good to be at sea. The last few days at home had been a sad time for the old king had died. He had been a great Viking in his day but on one voyage he had been half-blinded by a blow in battle and though he could see to do ordinary things he was no longer able to fight, so he had stayed at home and become old. It was said he was past forty when he died and it was terrible to see him for he was greatly crippled as well as half-blind. The scourge of Vikingia was this deadly illness which swelled the joints and bent the limbs. There was no cure and it was worst in wet weather; some old people were so bent it was impossible to straighten their limbs to put them into coffins when they died. A man should be killed in battle, particularly if he was a king. They had given the old king a royal burial; they had put his body in a ship with his weapons and gold, and silver, and all the things he would need in the next world and then they had burnt it. It was a strange and frightening scene; clouds of smoke had rolled around, the women were weeping and the men looked bored and uneasy. Suddenly the body had flung an arm upright. It was the heat of course but it had sent a wave of terror through the people. After a while the ashes and timbers had floated away out to sea and there was no trace. He wished the sea could wash away the traces from his memory as quickly and easily.

Suddenly there was a shout: someone had seen land. He was too occupied with the great steering oar to be able to look round but others could and when he was relieved from the oar he too saw it.

Nobody in the boat, not even Olaf, knew exactly where they were going. It was not England, where he had once been before. The way to England was known well enough but this time they had come much farther south. England had been raided so often that as like as not they would find the best plunder had been taken or burnt, if not safely hidden, nor was the opposite land much better, so they planned to slip through the neck of sea between the two countries and see what lay there. This land they could smell was England (it was in fact what is now East Anglia) so they kept on, the boat slicing eagerly through the waves, until they came to the mouth of a great river which was called Seine.

Into the Seine they turned and for a while they could still use the sail, then the water became too sheltered and they got out the oars. On and up they went. The narrow draught of their boats enabled them to venture far up shallow rivers; progress was swift, silent and deadly, for the inhabitants of the victim country had no idea of their arrival, still less that their own lives were in immediate danger. Now they found one of the streams, a tributary to the Seine. Soon it became shallow and muddy and, without wasting time, they pulled into the bank and moored the craft. It was now late afternoon, a good time for raiding. They were but one crew, twenty-four in all, but it was enough. The speed of Viking raids made their victims believe they were attacked by hundreds or even thousands and it was their mobility which created this deception. A hundred men could land in four or five boats, fan out, kill, burn, plunder, and re-embark, within an hour they were doing the same again far down the coast, and again later. By the time the local defences had been raised and the *burh* (local stronghold camp) manned, it was too late; the Vikings were miles away, ravaging and burning.

This time they crept ashore unseen. For a while rewards were few. They saw two villages where they raced in and killed those who did not manage to escape, screaming, from their long swords and whirling axes. They were poor places, fishing villages around which were a few straggly cattle and poor crops, but in the third the Vikings were lucky. Here there was grass and on it were horses. This was a fine sight; there is something about a horse; you can ride on it, you can eat it, you can even fight on it, for a horse will go to battle almost as readily as its rider. Within an hour the Vikings had captured them all and were setting out again. This time they knew they could drive deep into the heart of the country, reach the more prosperous places, kill and plunder and return to the ship.

And so it was. The horses were half wild and sometimes threw them but within a few miles they came upon a monastery. Here were a few monks working in the fields; inside was a small quantity of gold plate. It was a small, unimportant place but Olaf said there should be more gold and insisted they should look for it. The monks were very brave; Olaf killed some of them slowly to help them to talk but they did not pay much attention to his threats; they died talking, but not to him; it was as if they were speaking to someone else who was also there but whom Rolf could not see. Rolf was puzzled; these were not men of war but they were very, very brave. Olaf wasted much time here and then they rode on. Soon they realized they were approaching a small town; the countryside was richer, but a town was a large venture for one small raiding crew. Rolf did not speak; he had too little experience in these matters, but others did and said they should move away, attack some smaller place and return to the boat with their plunder; they were already overburdened with cloth and gold and silver ornaments. Olaf merely laughed at their protests. 'These town-dwellers are fat and rich and cowardly,' he said. 'We shall conquer them easily. Then we shall all be very rich.'

As they approached, Olaf's words did not seem to be true. The town had a broad ditch around it, three palisades of stakes and an earth rampart. On the rampart were sentries and there was much activity. It looked as if the Viking surprise was not complete. Perhaps one of those who had escaped from the first villages they had raided had reached here and given warning. Olaf had been a fool to waste so much time at the monastery. But Olaf was like a great bull, strong, fearless and thick-witted.

They circled around the palisades looking for a weak spot to attack. Nothing obvious showed itself. Rolf suddenly realized he was tired. Although he had taken his turn at sleep in the boat he had now been on the move since dawn when it had been his turn to take the steering-oar. For a fight such as this it seemed important that a man should feel rested and fresh. However if they waited that would give away the last chance of catching this town before it was fully prepared. It was certainly not the way Olaf saw the problem.

Rolf looked at his comrades and felt a surge of confidence. All were tall, fair, hard men. They swung their axes idly as if they were feathers. And there was Olaf. Olaf was redder, fiercer and more bull-like than ever.

'On men,' he shouted in his peculiar vibrating voice, which

half jarred and half excited. 'They have built a good wall round their town. It will serve to keep them in while we slaughter them all.'

With these words he moved forward. All Vikings had the *Berserkgangr* – the joy in battle – the only fear that any Viking felt was to die at home like the old king, with twisted painful limbs, and the only joy, above that of women and drinking, was to hurl yourself at the enemy, heaving, hacking, slashing, up to final victory. Sometimes men could not stop at the end of the fighting and would split open the dead enemy with an axe; it was called 'making an eagle'. Rolf thought that was stupid and pointless but he did not say so; he did not wish to be thought a weakling. But of all the Vikings none was as brave or mad as Olaf.

They ran quickly to follow him. Already he had reached the first palisade and was wrenching at the stakes. The enemy were throwing spears at him but he did not try either to dodge or to ward them off with his shield. Instead he wrenched at the stakes until he tore one away. Then, using that as a lever, he made an opening. In a second he was through, over the ditch – which was not deep – and into the next palisade. Soon others had followed his example and were hacking and wrenching at the stakes themselves. It was a true Viking attack. One moment they were standing wondering whether it was possible to capture the town, watched by the defenders who hoped and thought the Vikings might find it too difficult and go away; the next moment the invaders were nearly inside the barricades.

The defenders, who knew what to expect – bad news travels fast – were now converging on the breach. Slung stones, darts and spears rattled around Rolf. Magnus, the huge warrior from the northern fiord suddenly gave a great cry which ended in a choking gurgle. Rolf glanced sideways. A thrown spear had sliced half Magnus's neck away. Nor was he the only one to fall. For a moment the shock of Magnus's death, Magnus the un-conquerable, caused the Vikings to waver. But not Olaf. If Olaf had seen or heard it, it meant nothing. Olaf was mad with the joy of battle. Now at the rampart he was laughing wildly at the spears thrust at him. Disdaining his shield he clutched the sharp blades and while the blood streamed through his fingers pulled them away from their owners. It could not last; soon Olaf's hands were useless, perhaps for ever and he stood wildly bellowing: 'Come on you cowards, the town is won.'

The shock of seeing Olaf's plight sent a fresh wave of energy through the rest of the Vikings whose numbers were already reduced by seven. They gave the wild war cry which they always saved for the moment of defeat or victory and launched themselves forward. This time it was victory, but by the narrowest of margins. Ironically, it was the helpless Olaf who was the deciding factor. As he hurled himself forward, unarmed, unable to hold his shield, with blood spraying from him like a fountain, the defenders concentrated all their efforts to fell him. In a moment a dozen spears were sunk in his heaving body, but in the next second the rest of the Vikings were through and past him. Once across the rampart the rest was easy. The defenders still fought, but not all of them. If they had realized how few the Vikings were they could have rallied and not a Viking would have returned to the ship, but the speed and the shock of the attack had been too much. Soon all fighting stopped. The Vikings were looking for plunder of which there was a vast quantity and the defenders who had not been killed were lying up in their hiding places, eyeing with grim calculation the Viking depredations; more dangerous was the fact that, terrified though they were, they were now counting up the slender numbers of the Viking force.

For a while Rolf joined in the chasing and the slaughter and the ransacking, but this was not what he had come over the seas to find. Here was cloth and gold and silver; here were women – he could hear them screaming as the Vikings caught and raped them – but these were not what he wanted. Rolf wanted land; as he had ridden through this country on an abominable horse which had nearly split his crutch in half he had been thinking: if I lived here I could grow rich with this land. He thought of that small barren farm in Halden and suddenly his mind was made up.

As he paused for breath, leaning on his axe, he saw Sigvald, young, stupid Sigvald, take a burning piece of wood and put it to a thatch. It did not catch alight and Sigvald, cursing, turned to take another from the fire where some hapless defender had been cooking less than a half hour before. 'Stop', he said. 'Do not burn it. We must stay here.'

Sigvald turned and looked at him. 'Stay here?' he said. 'I shall not stay here. I shall burn it, take my plunder and return to Vikingia.' As he spoke the words he leered at Rolf like a treacherous dog. At the same time he twisted the handle of his axe so that the head whirled in a small circle. 'You are not chief,' he said. 'Olaf is chief.'

Rolf looked at him, taking in the loose, careless way Sigvald looked and talked. 'Olaf is dead,' he answered. 'We will speak with the others.'

For a moment Sigvald hesitated, wondering whether to try to fire the roof once more but realizing that if he once turned away he would be split in half by Rolf's axe, he waited. Rolf shouted the rallying cry which was usually only uttered by the leader. Soon the rest of the Vikings were around him. They were cut, blood-bespattered, wild; they looked like demons out of hell. The wretched survivors, cringing in their yet unburnt roof reeds, shuddered with uncontrollable fear. These were not men; they were evil spirits; no wonder resistance had been useless.

Rolf spoke: 'Olaf is dead,' he said. 'I am the eldest son of Leif the Brave. I am therefore your leader. I shall stay here and take land. Who will stay with me and be rich?'

There was a pause and muttering. Suddenly Sigvald spoke. 'Why should you be our leader? You are not the oldest or the strongest or the wisest. I shall not stay. Who will come back with me?'

He threw out his chin and stared in defiance at Rolf. Rolf was leaning lightly on his axe. Suddenly, before anyone could see what was happening he flung it upwards with the end of the handle towards Sigvald's neck. It caught him squarely. Sigvald gave a wild choking cry as the wooden handle split its way into his throat. Then he pitched forward and lay on the ground.

Rolf looked around the group. 'Sigvald will stay', he said, 'for ever, but he will never own land and be rich. Who will stay with me, and be owners of great tracts of land?'

Land. That was the word which made any Viking pause. War, women, drinking – but land. With land you could have them all. Each man's mind flickered back to the short growing season in the north, the small plots, the lack of fertile soil. Here it was otherwise; huge areas of land were theirs for the taking, fertile soil, fruit in abundance, and wine. Here too men came to trade, and goods which were rare possessions in Vikingia were here owned by all. Olaf would not have settled, Olaf was too restless and would have wandered on till he died as poor as he was born. Sigvald was half the warrior that Olaf was but he was just as lazy and pig-headed. At that moment Rolf suddenly sensed the changed pattern of his life. They would have land but by that decision they had suddenly become defenders and not attackers. Anyone could sail the seas, raid, fight, plunder and go, if not killed at any stage; they could rest when they were tired and fight when they wanted; now they would face a different task. The people here must not be slaughtered; they must be befriended and ruled. Property must not be burnt and destroyed but shared and added to. Women must not be raped but made into housewives and mothers of Viking sons.

All this went through Rolf's mind in a flash. Suddenly he noticed that the Vikings were looking to him, waiting for his next words. In that moment he realized that they were expecting orders, advice, praise or blame. He had become their leader. He would hold that position as long as he filled the part, as long as he thought ahead, solved problems, kept them under control. If not, he would soon suffer the fate of Sigvald.

'Good,' he said, taking their silence to be approval. 'Now these are my orders. Destroy nothing, and kill only those who resist or try to escape. First we shall eat, but not drink too much. Then we shall put out food for those who are alive and still hiding. Some will not come at first because they will think it a trap and that they will be killed; but others are greedy and stupid and will come. Soon all will come and they will know we are the masters for we control the food. But each night we shall keep watch just as we did on the sea. We are few in number, we may be attacked by treachery. Once other towns know we are here and that we are few in number they will send warriors to kill us. Tomorrow we must repair and strengthen the palisades. We shall make these people deepen the ditch. Then, when it suits us, we shall capture other towns. But remember this: now we are rich and soon we shall be richer; our numbers are small; make no mistake, others will try to take what we have, other Northmen will find their way here. We shall make these people work and fight for us, our work will be fighting our enemies and making our people work; that is the future. Now we shall eat.'

As he stopped speaking he looked over the heads and saw the sun well down in the sky. That day he had seen it rise out of the sea when he was but one of a crew of raiders; now he was a landowner and a chief. Other warriors had had similar days but few had kept their gains. He would be one of the few who held what had been taken.

Rolf and his men survived. They were lucky in that they were able to settle down before they had to fight for their lives. Their worst enemies were the wine which made them quarrel among themselves and the easiness of their lives which made them lazy. Nevertheless when they were attacked by other wandering bands of Northmen, as the local people called them, they managed to fight them off. Part of their success was due to Rolf's idea of building a huge mound of earth which wandering bands of adventurers could not climb easily or quickly to attack. Faced with such a formidable obstacle, enemies usually sheered off and looked for easier targets.

Rolf had been born in AD 827. He had arrived in Seine Inferieure with his Northmen, who soon became known as the Normans, in 847. Ten years later his township and estate had become part of a wider structure of settlement. Towards the end of the ninth century Rolf's descendants took part in the sack of Paris. The Vikings were bought off here but they ravaged far and wide elsewhere. Only in England had the all-conquering Norsemen been checked but even there success was only partial.

But Rolf's settlement survived; the price of survival was constant readiness for war. When the town became part of the Dukedom of Normandy there was always fighting to do, mainly against Bretons or men of Anjou. Fighting, or preparation for warfare, became such a customary activity that the Normans were bored and restless when not on the battlefield.

In 1066 the head of Rolf's family went with William the Conqueror to England. With his followers was an archer named Bowman who fought at the Battle of Hastings. After the battle he was transferred to the army of another feudal lord, William Fitzosbern.

BOWMAN
The Norman Archer

Bowman's eye travelled meditatively along the far bank of the Wye. It was well within range. From his post on the north-east corner of the Great Tower he could cover fifty paces of that bank. He fingered the new weapon proudly and possessively. There were not a dozen like it in the country. It was a revolution in warfare; if there were enough of them made it would probably make war impossible.

It was a new idea, this weapon. It was said to have been invented in Sicily where the Normans had found it a year or two before. The southern people did not use it properly; they shot at too long a range and then panicked and threw it away when the Normans came to close-quarters. Even the Normans did not see its possibilities at first. They believed the proper way to win battles was by hacking away with the broadsword. Well, that certainly produced results; they not only won their battles but they chopped their opponents in pieces as well. The knights set no store by slung stones or arrows; they despised them as women's weapons.

Well, a few would learn differently today, thought Bowman. This new, secret weapon would cut down a knight or his horse before he even saw what was coming. He was proud of his crossbow, as it was called: instead of pulling the bow with the strength in your arms you used a lever called 'a goat's foot'; that way you could draw a bigger, stronger bow and use greater power. Bowman was right in his opinion of his new toy; within fifty years it was to create such devastation among the knights that the Pope had it banned for use against Christian nations.*

But the crossbow looked like being the only good feature of today, and when they lost – as they would – he would need to get rid of it fast. People using new, deadly weapons tend to be very roughly handled when captured; being killed was one thing, being tortured, blinded or burnt was another.

This, thought Bowman, looked like the end of the road. His feudal lord, young Roger of Breteuil, had taken arms against

* The Lateran Edict of 1139.

the mighty Conqueror. It was said to be some quarrel over taxes. Some of the younger soldiers had been very excited when it had begun but Bowman felt that it was madness for the barons to quarrel with the king just when they were settling a new country and were surrounded on all sides by enemies, but the barons were like that and if you were in a baron's service his quarrel was your cause.

Not that Bowman minded a fight: he loved it. He had been brought up in the castle of William de Varenne in Bellencombre. William was a mighty baron, and was known as the Companion of the Conqueror. Bowman had come with him to England, landed at Hastings, and fought in the great battle nine years ago. It was all a dim memory now, though certain incidents were as fresh as the day they had occurred. He had carried a short bow then; it was a despised weapon but it had turned the day in the great battle when hour after hour they had tried to break the Saxon shield wall. Nobody really knew what had happened though afterwards everybody gave a description of every stage of the battle as if it had been quite orderly. He himself had been completely confused; for a long time he was doing nothing, then, all at once, it seemed as if everyone on the Saxon side was trying to reach him. Then, after a short desperate fight in which he killed men who were not fighting him at all and was nearly killed by others whom he did not see until they aimed blows at him and missed, he was isolated again. At the end they chased the Saxons but were nearly ambushed themselves. Afterwards, because most of William Fitzosbern's men had been killed in the battle he was transferred from William de Varenne and made a man-at-arms in the service of William Fitzosbern. He did not like it but had no choice. He would have preferred to stay with William de Varenne who was now one of the greatest barons in England. It was said that all William de Varenne's soldiers were his kinsmen, children by *droit de seigneur*, and a man felt pride in serving in such a community, under a lord who was said to be the most valiant of all the barons. However, a soldier goes where he is sent and that is all there is to it. Fitzosbern had been made Earl of Hereford; there were Normans in those parts before the Conquest and they were well hated. On the way to Hereford they had built two motte and bailey castles; as they had moved westwards Fitzosbern had encountered many hostile groups and was apprehensive that there might be a great army coming from Devon and Cornwall. The technique of building a motte was simple enough; you rounded up as many of the local people as you could find and then encircled them while they built a great mound. Most of the earth for the mound came from the ditches at the base but some had to be carried farther. It was essential to have a lot of labourers for not only did it quicken the task but their feet also trampled the earth firm. It was remarkable how a few jabs with a sword helped them along.

Fitzosbern did not stay long at Hereford and immediately began building a castle at Chepstow, or Striguil, as the Welsh called it. This was a proper lord's castle, not a mere earth motte and bailey; Fitzosbern had brought over masons from Normandy and they supervised the quarrying of the stone and the building. The Great Tower was the finest castle anywhere, he thought, although travellers said the White Tower at London was even better. It was a great, long building overlooking the river Wye with a valley known as the Dingle separating it from the township. It took five years to build and Bowman's task was to protect the workmen from Welsh raids. After two years they had cleared the countryside of all hostile Welsh and most of the soldiers, like himself, had taken local wives. His was a small, dark-eyed woman, like the Breton women. She had borne two sons and he now felt more content and settled than he had ever done. Perhaps he was getting old – he had passed thirty – and he was happy to be left on castle-guard with one of these new secret weapons. But one day that settled life had exploded; William Fitzosbern had died and been succeeded by his son, wild Roger of Breteuil. Roger had never accepted the Conqueror as his feudal overlord who could tax him, but only as a partner in the enterprise of overrunning England. Ralf, Earl of

Norfolk, shared his view and together they decided to rebel and put Waltheof, an old Saxon noble, in the Conqueror's place. But the Conqueror had been too quick and too clever for them; Ralf had already fled overseas and Roger had fallen back to Chepstow. And here he was on 20 August 1075, waiting for the Conqueror's final attack. It was said that the king had blinded all Norfolk's soldiers as an example and had threatened worse when he came here: a man would be a fool if he let himself be captured alive.

From his watchpost on the Great Tower Bowman noted the frenzied activity still going on below. There was very little danger of a storming party coming up the west side, and none at all of anyone crawling up the north bank. The danger lay on the east side where men were even now trying to deepen the ditches – an almost impossible task in the rock – and to build more barricades. All around him on the top of the tower were stones, and cauldrons for boiling water and heating sand red-hot. There was quicklime too. When men tried to batter in the doorway a shower of quicklime and red-hot sand in the eyes had a fine effect. There was water up here too for quenching fires which might be started. Out in the bailey Roger and his commanders were rushing round telling men to do half a dozen jobs at once. The work was all being done by soldiers; the Welsh who did most of the rough work around the castle in normal times had suddenly disappeared.

It fell to Bowman to strike the first blow. Suddenly one of the king's knights came to the bank on the far side of the Wye and took a long cool look at the defences. Clearly his job was to report back and equally clearly it never crossed his mind he could be in any sort of danger, but Bowman had him lined up exactly on his crossbow and suddenly the knight gave a great leap in his saddle and slowly slid to the ground. The crossbow bolt had ripped its way into his chest taking the chain mail with it. Bowman grinned at the accuracy and strength of his shot. Almost as the knight fell two others came up to the same point. They bent over the dead man and looked around, puzzled, then, leading his horse, they quickly disappeared back into the trees. Bowman did not take a second shot.

There was a pause for an hour, a very tense hour. No one else appeared on the far bank although figures could be seen dimly moving among the trees; then even that movement stopped.

Just before midday there was a sudden sharp attack on the outer barricade of the east bailey. The enemy appeared very swiftly and launched a swarm of burning arrows into the piled brushwood. As the defenders rushed to pour water on the blazing thorns other archers found them easy targets. Clearly arrows were being used much more than they had been in the past; perhaps the success at Hastings had caused that. The pressure of the attack seemed to be mounting steadily but it did not seem very wholehearted. Suddenly he realized why. There were screams from the west side and shouts. 'Look out', he heard. 'The main attack is coming here.'

Now Roger showed that not only was he an ambitious fool but also an incompetent commander. As Bowman launched crossbow bolts at the knights he could see close to the east barricade, Roger was detaching men and telling them to go to the west side. The result was that both sides of the castle were weak at once, and to make matters worse there came another shout: 'Look to the north. They are coming down the river too.'

He looked; there were three boats only. Obviously the men he had seen through the trees had been working their way up river to where there were boats. This was his task. Using the bolt he had planned for a huge knight with a green dragon on his shield he turned reluctantly to the river. Aiming just below the water line of the first boat he sent the bolt straight and true. For a moment nothing seemed to have happened; then with a grim satisfaction he saw the boat fill with water and overturn. Its occupants sank like stones. All were wearing mail. Had they been wearing leather jerkins and a metal cap like he was they might have had a chance of swimming to the shore; sometimes it was no advantage to be rich enough to buy armour.

Before he could reload, the other two boats had landed at the base of the cliff on the north side. There was no one to stop them now. Bowman was no military tactician but he doubted whether that main attack could be coming from the west side. The king's men would have had to have skirted right round the town and through the woods to mount it. Some knights were very clever and it seemed they could read the enemy's mind and guess his every intention; the king was one of them. Yes, thought Bowman to himself, I am only a common crossbowman and no one has ever thought of asking me my opinion but I suspect that this is a double feint. He looked for the knight with the green dragon on his shield but he was no longer there.

But others were. As he feared, the east was where the main attack would fall. From his viewpoint he could see a solid mass of knights and men-at-arms charging at the barricades; men were falling, fire was beginning to take hold; he was curiously detached from it all. Suddenly he heard a voice behind him: 'All down and help at the east bailey.'

He slung his bow on his back, dropped his last bolt back in the quiver and loosened his sword in the scabbard; then he ran down. At ground level it was a very different picture. As he moved up through the smoke to the barricade one of the king's soldiers came leaping through and stumbled; Bowman had his sword in the man's throat even before either of them realized it; it was pure instinct. As the man fell another followed but he was cut down by one of the castle knights who was fighting dismounted. It was a hopelessly confused scene; you could not know whether you were winning or losing, where your side were or what you should do. He wounded another man, whom someone else finished off with a wild, sweeping stroke. Now there was yet another shout: 'Back to the tower. Hold the tower.'

Who gave the order he did not know but it was obviously a commander's voice. He raced up the ladders and once more reached the battlement. To his dismay there were only three others with him; the rest were either dead, lost, or had not heard the order. He looked down. He could make nothing of the scene below in the swirling smoke; the barricades were all alight; on the far side he could see the ranks of the king's men waiting to plunge in the moment the smoke cleared. None of those who had come up with him was a sergeant or a knight. It was obvious that three men could not defend the Great Tower. This was the worst battle he had ever fought in; there was either no direction or wrong orders, but he had no option but to wait. The smoke thinned a little down below and they peered as best they could through it. What they saw was no comfort.

By now it was clear that the battle was lost. The huts in the bailey were all burning and the smoke from them drifted in clouds over the castle. Here and there he could see small groups of men fighting; it was always one against several and the one was, of course, a Chepstow man.

Now was the time to go, if it were not already too late. This was the very worst point in a battle, when your own side was hopelessly defeated and your leaders were either dead or had made their escape leaving you to your fate and as like as not all escape routes had been blocked. Nevertheless the clouds of smoke gave some hope; with luck he might plunge right through and emerge on the far side. Still clutching his crossbow with only one bolt left he ran quickly towards the thick smoke in the west bailey. Two of the enemy saw him and swung to intercept him but he was past them and into the smoke.

This was a different form of agony. His eyes streamed, his throat and lungs filled with choking smoke and his legs seemed to buckle beneath him, but somehow he staggered on. If he met an enemy on the other side he was doomed for he would hardly have the strength to raise his arm. Suddenly he was clear; there were enemy soldiers around but they did not notice him in the swirling confusion of the billowing smoke which they themselves seemed trying to avoid. In a moment he was past them and sliding down into the west ditch. He staggered and stumbled away to the left along the Dingle, gradually making his way up the slope into the woodland. He was suddenly aware how quiet everything had become; behind in the castle there was a confused noise, crackling of burning wood and occasional shouts and screams. It reminded him he had not gone far, but he paused a moment to recover his breath. The most dangerous moment was still to come. Now, more cautiously he began to work his way back to the town – to his house where his wife and boys would be hiding. He had no fears that the enemy would have found them; he had often admired the swift resourcefulness with which this Welsh woman could anticipate danger and keep out of the way of harm. Even now a thought of pride in the future of his sons crossed his mind. The mixture of the hard Norman soldier and the agile alert Welsh stock would make great soldiers; perhaps they would become knights.

The town was unharmed. That was undoubtedly the Conqueror's order. He was teaching his rebel barons a lesson, not terrorizing the countryside. The Conqueror could spread terror when he chose but a hard man like that also had a grip on his own troops. He must have given orders to kill the castle garrison but leave the townsfolk alone.

The streets were empty apart from a few children. No doubt a herald had come earlier in the day and told everyone to keep inside their homes. As he moved swiftly to his own home he felt the place reeked of the sour smell of defeat. He himself felt a leper, even though nobody had fought harder and better than he had that day.

The door of his house was open, which was unexpected. In a second he was inside. To his astonishment there was no one there. He looked around, bewildered; for a moment he did not take it in then gradually, like a returning pain, began to realize what had happened. They had gone, his wife, the boys, and their clothes; the house was bare. Puzzled, he noticed they had also taken the cooking pots and his own old swords. They must be waiting for him somewhere, but where?

Suddenly a shadow blocked the doorway, and he jerked abruptly back to reality. But it was only a boy, the son of a neighbour. Well, perhaps he knew something or had a message. The boy looked at him curiously, in a calculating way as if wondering if he could betray him. 'Where are my family?' Bowman snapped at him. 'Have you seen them?'

The boy looked at him contemptuously as if this was a foolish question. 'They left this morning,' he said. 'Emrys took them.'

Emrys? Bowman's mind reeled. 'Emrys!' he almost choked over the name. He recalled the dark, swarthy features of Emrys the tanner, who used to bring them little leather presents, purses and the like. Bowman despised the man and told his wife not to accept them but she had laughed and asked what was the harm in it. She was sorry for Emrys, whose wife was openly unfaithful to him.

'Yes, Emrys,' the boy went on calmly. 'I was listening when he came. He said you would never come back and the king's men would kill them.' He stopped, then went on. 'He was a good friend to them. He was always here when you were on castle guard and he used to help your wife when she went to gather berries and faggots in the woods. They will never come back now.'

Bowman looked at the child, who seemed to be taking some pleasure in the news he was giving. He jerked his head at him. 'Be off,' he said. Surprised the boy scuttled away.

Well, said Bowman to himself, it's my own fault and I've myself only to blame. Once a man puts down roots, once he entrusts his happiness to someone instead of to the wine flask and the battle he is a man plunging into the fight without a shield. It is not the right way for a soldier, not the right way at all. There is only one way for a soldier.

Drawing his sword, he noticed the dried blood on it. He had forgotten that: it seemed so long ago. Then, sharply, he ripped it across the strings of his beloved crossbow. He hacked at the notch till it was useless and putting the goat's foot lever under his foot pulled it out of shape. Nobody would be able to repair it now, even if they understood what it was. Still holding his sword he moved to the door. The streets were still deserted but

over the castle larger clouds of smoke were billowing into the
sky. Smiling confidently he began to walk towards it.

The boy had been right. Bowman's wife and sons never did
come back to Chepstow. Emrys always had a lurking fear that
Bowman might still be alive and would find them so they
moved right up into Powys where they lived in fear of the armies
of the quarrelsome Welsh princes. The boys despised Emrys
although their mother told them he had rescued them from the
Normans when their father had been killed; they did not believe
Emrys could rescue anyone. They became very skilled with the
Welsh longbow and often ambushed the Normans who were
forcing their way up into Central Wales. Their sons were no less
skilful and took great delight in harassing the Norman outposts
at Whitecastle and Abergavenny. Towards the end of the
twelfth century one of their descendants joined the forces of the
Earl of Hereford as a mercenary. His name was Gawain.

GAWAIN

The Crusader

Gawain felt as if he had been here in the Holy Land all his life. In fact, although he knew at the back of his mind that he belonged to another country where there were soft, green woods and a broad, cool river, it seemed so far away and long ago that it was as unreal as the mirages which constantly tormented the soldiers. He reminded himself that Hereford was his home and if he ever got back there the cool waters would wash the dust and sand out of his eyes, his skin would lose its dried, rough look and he would begin to feel free again; but in another sense he was almost afraid to go back. This hard light, the sweat, the ferocity and cruelty of man as well as of nature had become so much a part of his life that he was not at all sure what would happen when he left it. Accustomed misery is sometimes a comforting companion. A man feels he knows the worst and that is better than the unknown. Still, it would be pleasant to be able to take the armour off for long enough for the limbs to straighten and the sores to heal.

It was 12 May 1192, although Gawain did not know it. It was just another day, or so he thought. Day followed day out here and would always do so. His horse stumbled and without thinking he steadied it and lapsed back into his thoughts. Within a few hours they would be at Jerusalem which they must capture, whatever the odds; then with the Holy City in their hands that would be the time for rewards; then he would be granted English lands to which his rank now entitled him, but which he did not possess. The Holy City had been taken and made into a Christian kingdom a hundred years before but a few years ago it had been lost again and now their own Crusade was going to win it back. They were led by the great Richard the Lionheart. There was a man for a soldier to follow! He would plunge into the fight with his great battleaxe, scorning the protection his rank provided. There was nothing a soldier could do which he could not do better. Even so, Gawain was a little uneasy when he was confronted by King Richard. Although the king had married in Cyprus he did not seem interested in women, like most of the army; he would put his hand on your face when he spoke to you. It made Gawain shudder, yet the king was a great soldier, and they needed great soldiers; so many had been killed or died, dried out by the heat, but those who were left were as hardened as he was. As he stumbled on through the sand his mind wandered back and forth. When he looked up he could see Richard's entourage plodding ahead. On each side of him were other groups of bannerets, stretching out to be lost in the haze. It was dangerous to peer into the glare so he lowered his eyes and let his mind wander back.

Three years had passed since he set out on this Crusade, and what a way he had come in that time! It was not merely a matter of distance but of status. Three years ago he had been an archer in the service of the Earl of Hereford. Although only twenty-three he commanded a *herce*, which at Hereford was eighteen men; the word really meant the triangular formation which archers took up in battle but they used it as a command unit. Nobody quite knew what to make of Gawain and the thought amused him. He was obviously half Welsh and that alone would have made him distrusted in Hereford but he also understood the Normans and the English. Nobody took any liberties with Gawain. With sling, arrow, spear or dart he could outdistance them all, and he could tumble any man on his back if he seemed to be making too much of himself. Others drew swords and put men in prison, but not Gawain, he never needed to; he had never had to punish a man yet but nobody wanted to be the first. He could also make weapons, or find a way when others were lost. His father had been like him but his father had taken one chance too many in stabbing a wild boar.

Gawain had had no idea what a Crusade was until he found himself on it. Even now the early part seemed a dream. There had been all the preparations: the arrows, the horseshoes, the armour and then the sea journey to France where they had marched to Gisors to a vast field with an old Saxon cross in it. This was the assembly point and it was here that, in spite of the priests and the blessings, Gawain began to have doubts about the religious motives of those who were taking part. It was said that many were merely there to save themselves damnation for a lifetime of sins, and they looked it; nor did they look as if repentance had begun. Apart from the soldiers there was a vast host of camp followers, beggars, tinkers, drabs, vagabonds. He had a problem keeping his men out of trouble, scuffles, dagger fights. Sometimes there were quarrels with other English or French; sometimes they fell out over the scummy women. He saw Philip Augustus of France and did not trust him and the Lionheart probably did not either, but they went through a marvellous ceremony at Nonancourt in which the two kings swore enough oaths of allegiance and made enough plans for twenty Crusades. Then all set off to Sicily and had to spend the winter there.

At that time they had been on the Crusade for two years and were not more than half-way to their goal. There was nothing to do but to quarrel with the French and by all accounts that was what the Lionheart was also doing. Two years: sometimes he thought of his wife and family; perhaps they had already forgotten him, or never expected to see him again. They would be surprised if they did for that winter of 1190 the Lionheart had arranged all sorts of tournaments and contests. In one Gawain's *herce* had been matched against the French: they had thrown, ridden, wrestled and crossed swords with them and each time Gawain's men had won. The Lionheart was so pleased he had knighted Gawain on the spot; even then Gawain did not like him. So if his family ever saw Gawain again they would find him a knight. But he was a realist; without land and money a knighthood meant little; you could not eat a coat of arms.

This burning heat was a test men seldom encountered. Life was always producing a fresh challenge. Gawain recalled the peculiar embarrassing ceremonials in Cyprus when the Lionheart had married Queen Berengaria. This was not his world and he knew it; if all that falsity and show went with high rank he never wanted to reach it. Acre had been a more familiar scene. For two years the town had been under siege, but the sight that had astonished them had been the condition of the besiegers, not the besieged. So great had been their losses through privation the previous winter that it was clear that they would never have taken the town had the English not arrived. Conditions could be bad inside a town but they were sometimes infinitely worse outside where the besiegers had little shelter, uncertain food supplies and a gradually diminishing force. Sometimes the besieged would sally out and scatter half the besiegers, who were also themselves partly besieged. To make matters worse, the two leaders, Guy de Lusignan and Conrad de Montferrat, were quarrelling over who should be king of Jerusalem when they retook it. Of course, Richard and Philip Augustus joined in, supporting opposite sides. Then both fell ill with fevers. Richard was the first to recover and soon broke into the walls with the catapult ammunition he had brought with him. These flint-hard stones, some weighing 100 lbs each, would either smash a piece of wall or themselves disintegrate into a mass of flying fragments; one of the latter had killed twelve Saracens at once. Although the French failed to mine the wall properly and the Saracens were attacking behind the English lines, the besieged were so exhausted that they surrendered; then there were stupid and bad-tempered massacres by both sides. Philip Augustus said he was too ill to continue and went home, doubtless to plan fresh treachery. The army moved on to Jaffa. It was a terrible journey, slow and exhausting; the Saracens attacked them at Arsouf but the Crusaders were so full of pent-up fury they had cut the enemy to pieces. It was a marvellous victory; he smiled as he thought of it. They had spent the winter at Jaffa and it had been bitterly cold. Richard had had the army at work rebuilding the fortifications and the men used to joke, saying: 'This will make it twice as hard to retake when next we lose it.' Probably they were right. Gawain had lived with a Saracen woman there and when they left to press on to Jerusalem the next year she was carrying his child. What a mixture he will be, thought Gawain. I am a mixture myself and I don't doubt that his mother is. Still he'll probably be no worse for that.

When they pressed on towards Jerusalem it had suddenly become very hot, dry and dusty. Everyone knew that this was the most dangerous moment of the whole expedition. Not only was their army too small for a successful attack on the large and well-defended city but it was known that the mighty Saladin had a great Saracen army in the hills, waiting to attack them when they were spread thinly round Jerusalem. But you don't win wars by avoiding risks and clearly Richard had decided to make the gamble. Gamble it was, for morale in the army was low, co-operation hardly existed and most of the barons felt that this Crusade had gone on too long already. Everybody knew what happened when barons went off on Crusades, their servants at home robbed them, their neighbours overran some of their land and the wives – well, that was a story in itself. None of it seemed to matter in the early days when honour and glory and riches and adventure and salvation seemed in prospect but after three years of hardship, frustration and failure men began to think of home and not sentimentally either.

For his part, Gawain did not much mind what happened; he was extremely uncomfortable at the moment and perhaps matters would get worse. So far he had been scarcely troubled by the fevers that had struck down so many of the others but he was a little uneasy lest this heat should bring one on. For him the Crusade had been a story of continued success, although somehow it gave him no pleasure; perhaps that would come later. He was now a banneret, and if three years ago a prophet had told him he would become a banneret he would have laughed aloud. But in the battle of Arsouf, when they had put the Saracens to rout, he had caught Richard's eye again and been elevated to being a knight-banneret. He commanded thirty men-at-arms, including twelve of the original *herce* (the rest were all dead) and he even had two knights-bachelor under him. Knights-bachelor were poor knights – *bas chevaliers* – who had planned to make their fortune but had usually lost the little

58

they started with. One was very dull and spoke slowly and indistinctly; Gawain thought he must have had a blow on the head at some time and had his brain damaged. The other was good in battle but had too high an opinion of himself; the men hated him, and he despised them. He was called Sir Guy de Tilleul and could never forget it. Both these carried pennons, as Gawain had once done, but when he had been made a banneret Richard had cut the point off the pennon and made it a banner. Well, it would all be fine if he lived to tell the tale.

The army was now moving very slowly. It seemed to fill the whole plain but he knew it was probably outnumbered by the Saracens. Tomorrow it would be his turn to protect the flanks, moving up and down the column looking for the enemy. It would be hard work but more interesting than just staying in column. He was in full mail armour, but like all the other knights he had taken off his great pot helmet which fitted right over his head and came down to his shoulders; it now hung by the high pommel of his saddle. Mail was heavy for it consisted of thousands of links beaten together and it had to be worn over a jerkin, but it was always worn on the march. Everything, sword, dagger, shield, seemed heavier in this heat. But in time you became used to everything. The greatest surprise had been how clean your skin kept even when you could not wash it. For the first few days, when there was no water for washing, the skin became dirtier and dirtier; then after a while you noticed your hands were clean again; the skin seemed to have a way of cleaning itself after a time. He would never have known that if he had not come out here.

The army seemed to be moving more slowly than ever. This, of course, was how it felt at the front. He had no doubt that at the rear men could hardly keep up. It was an extraordinary thing about large numbers of men on the march; the ones at the front seemed to be moving at a snail's pace but those at the back almost had to run to keep up; it was a mystery.

On his head, in place of his helmet, he wore a cloth cape, copied from the Saracens. Its folds stretched down over his neck protecting the part where the sun's rays seemed to bite most fiercely. Over his back he had another cape which covered his armour and prevented the links soaking up too much heat from the sun's rays. He was undoubtedly cooler than the men-at-arms who wore thick leather jerkins, tough enough to stop an arrow or dart but murderously hot in this sun. From time to time he passed his eye over them; all seemed well except one; that one was a big Hungarian who had joined them in Jaffa. Somehow he had become separated from his original company and had fallen in with Gawain's troop, but Gawain could make little of him. He drank, boasted and fought like the others but he never seemed one of them. They were a ragged enough collection but you could understand them and make them understand you. The Hungarian was different; there was no real contact. He was now rolling slightly in his walk but he would survive. Gawain turned to the front and forgot him.

On they went. It did not seem possible that the day could become hotter. There was a slight wind but all it did was whip up the sand and drive it against your skin. Suddenly he was alert. The army was stopping; orders were being shouted back from the Lionheart's group; he passed them on; the army stopped.

Suddenly there was a murmur of sound. It was men all asking each other what was happening. Nobody, of course, knew. Then from various quarters, barons came riding swiftly up to the Lionheart's concourse. Gawain was trying to penetrate the glare and see what was happening. He knew that he would be summoned with all the other knights-banneret if there was anything to be done; meanwhile they waited.

If it had been hot moving it was twice as bad standing still. He tried to look cool and calm but after a while a confused noise and shouting made him turn round; it was the Hungarian, he was mumbling and occasionally shouting words which no one understood. Gawain ignored him but he felt there might be trouble coming.

Up in front he could now see there were a number of French

and there seemed to be an argument between the barons. The heat was now like a great woollen blanket. He thought of the Wye and cool woods, and felt better. Men who had no memories and who could think neither of past nor future could not stand such conditions. But a lot of things could send men mad in the heat, too much wine was one.

Suddenly the Hungarian went mad; screaming he was pushing forward whirling his sword round his head. There was only one thing to be done and Gawain did it. He pulled his horse round, touched the spur and was right behind the raving man-at-arms; then swiftly and neatly he drove the point of his long dagger right into the man's neck. As the man collapsed the dagger was pulled out of Gawain's hands. Gawain felt neither pity nor sorrow; it was the only thing to do.

At that moment came fresh orders. The bannerets were summoned to Richard. As he moved forward he noticed some of the barons riding away back to their own armies. As he came to the Lionheart's position he was joined by many others. Richard paid no attention to them at first: he seemed to be brooding.

Then he spoke. 'We shall return,' he said. 'We shall retreat to Ascalon. The French refuse to continue and are withdrawing their army. Perhaps we shall come again. If we continue we shall be defeated, but if we retreat now we can obtain honourable treaties from Saladin.'

It was a tense moment. They were standing on a little hill. Suddenly the haze lifted and a knight, not perhaps remembering where he was, called out: 'Look, there is the Holy City.'

Gawain followed his gaze. There, where the heat haze had temporarily lifted, they could see Jerusalem, the Holy City. It was like a dream city, floating on the haze. That was Jerusalem.

Suddenly he was recalled by a wild cry. It was the Lionheart. He had snatched up his cloak and was holding it before his eyes. 'If I cannot conquer it', he said, 'I will not look on it.' And then he turned away.

In spite of the heat Gawain felt a little shudder run through his flesh. It was a sad moment but what a fool's gesture. And then it was finished. The army was turning and retreating. The Crusade was over – and lost.

Gawain's subsequent history does not concern us here. His child, whom he never saw, was a girl. She was brought up in Jaffa among many other children of mixed blood. When she was sixteen she had a son. When that son was thirty he had a daughter. It was of no interest to him, but when the girl was eighteen she was very beautiful; she was also intelligent. Not many people learn as they go along, but the girl, whose name was Munira, was wise and knew that places and people change.

BORU

The Mongol Warrior

On 1 August 1260 Boru was feeling reasonably pleased with himself. It was not his nature to feel content unless he was moving fast or fighting but there was a prospect of each in the near future and that, taken with everything else, removed the customary scowl from his flat features. Boru was no beauty: his body was squat and rather fat, his legs were short and he waddled as much as walked; at the best his face looked calmly impassive, at the worst, as when he was in battle, it looked positively demoniac. Like the other Mongols he created fear wherever he went. There was every reason for men to shudder when the Mongols were mentioned. They were swift, devastating, ruthless, treacherous, and cruel; they were seemingly unconquerable in warfare and even in the peace which eventually succeeded a ferocious and cruel campaign they were regarded as dangerous and unpredictable, yet those who came to know them realized that they were more than ruthless killers and that they had a peculiar morality of their own.

The woman Munira was one who knew this; her first meeting with Boru had been surprising, though memorable. Even as a child she had heard frightening stories of the Mongols who were relentlessly driving towards them. They had already conquered Iran. Men and women who had fled before them, or even seen them and later escaped, left no one in doubt of what a Mongol conquest was like. There were terrible stories: in one town they had cut off the heads of all the conquered and made a pile like a mountain; in another they had tied the people together and burnt them alive. The stories related not to one place but to many and they were all true. After Iran their path had not been so easy for then they had met the Turks – the Saracens, as they were called here – who had already defeated great armies of crusaders. Although nobody knew it at the time, the Turks had once come in a conquering horde from the same distant parts of the east as the Mongols. In time the former would prove the more lasting conquerors, and reach areas beyond the Mongol empire. Munira sensed this but it did not alter her feelings for Boru.

When the Mongols had swept into Palestine Munira had
been living in a small village on the frontier of what is now
Iraq. There was nowhere to flee to, no place where the Mongols
might not reach out and find you; therefore, like all the villagers
in the path of the dreaded invader they had hidden beneath
straw or in rubbish, hoping the Mongols would think they had
all fled. Later when the danger seemed to have passed they
would emerge and gradually find employment in the rear of
the Mongol army. There was a danger in hiding in the
huts for sometimes the Mongols burnt every village in their
path. If the wretched villagers tried to escape the flames the
Mongols would either pick them up and toss them back in, or
perhaps hold them at spear point as they tried to run out.
However, in times of danger risks are taken daily and there is
no time to think what would be the best course, so they had
stayed.

Munira had hidden under a pile of rubbish composed of
wool and old skins. It was hot and unpleasant but it was not
the sort of hiding place to draw attention. What she did not
know was that the Mongol drive was slowing down. Already
that day they had suffered losses and when they reached the
village were looking for shelter and a place where they could
re-form and obtain new horses. The Mongols therefore did not
thunder through the village spreading havoc when they arrived;
they stopped and found accommodation. Boru, who had a
command of ten men, came straight to Munira's hut, where her
father and mother and younger brother were also hiding. As
they burst through the doorway she crouched lower, half-
paralysed with fear; Boru walked to the bundle of rubbish and
flicked over the top skin with his sword; at that point Munira
could bear it no longer and stood up.

Boru's reaction was immediate. As the heap moved he stepped
back, sword at the ready, waiting to drive it home into what
emerged. To his astonishment there appeared a young, frightened but undoubtedly very shapely woman. For a second he
stood there, then taking a stride forward he seized her with one

hand and ripped at her clothes with the other. Then he flung himself on to her.

To her dying day Munira would never forget that moment; to her dying day too she would wear the scars made by Boru's iron spurs on her bare legs; then it was all over. The hut was full of Boru's soldiers who had witnessed such scenes too often before to be even more than faintly amused.

And that could have been the end of that. It was not, however. Munira wondered for a moment if she would now be killed. Instead she was ignored. She watched Boru give orders to his men. Most of them were not Mongols but from Turkmen, near the Caspian where they had been recruited into the Mongol army. When she recovered her wits she clutched her torn clothes around her and tried to leave. Boru saw her and motioned her to stay. Then he gave orders to kill her parents and brother; it was soon done.

That was a month ago, and in that time she had stayed with the Mongols and become Boru's woman. She had been made to work, but all the Mongol women worked just as hard. As she was Boru's woman no one tried to molest her; even when everyone became very drunk she felt safe. Their favourite drink was fermented mare's milk which made you drunk quickly; their food consisted mainly of meat, some of it horseflesh from mounts which were unlikely to be of much future use, but they also ate goat meat and cheese and drank mare and goat's milk. Much of her time was taken up with preparing this food.

It was obvious to Munira as soon as she began to look around that the Mongols had had a sharp battle just before they arrived; they were short of horses, and much of their equipment was damaged; many of the weapons were blunt and notched, and these were resharpened and repaired first. She realized that this was the spearhead of an attack, for within days a great host came to the village and set up their tents. They brought with them great war engines, catapults and rams, all carried by slaves. It was clear that this was not merely a string of desert nomads with fast ponies but an army which could besiege cities.

She studied Boru closely. He seemed to endure the heat of the day and chill of the night without feeling it. She had heard that the Mongol skin was different from that of other people, being very thick and not sweating much. Perhaps it was the result of centuries of hard living in extreme climates. She found they could understand each other's speech but she could seldom understand his mind. He seemed merely to be waiting. She wondered whether he would take her with him when he left. Other women were allowed to follow their men; they came along with the siege engines and stores. Being the wife to a Mongol was like being a favoured slave. He left her in no doubt about her duties: when he was out practising manoeuvres with his men, racing their tough little ponies wildly at each other then swinging away before the collision, she was checking and repairing his equipment; her duties even included examining the long lariat which hung by his saddle; if it were torn or frayed it was her task to splice or bind it and it was a hard assignment for a woman's fingers. In spite of his dependence on her at that moment she noted gloomily how self-contained he was; he carried two bows, and the material to repair them; he even had a skin bag which would be inflated when he required extra buoyancy in crossing rivers with his horse and equipment. It was well known that the Mongols usually rode their horses till they dropped, then cut steaks off them, put these under the saddle of the remount and rode on. Now, however, they were having to be more careful of their supplies, both of meat and horses. Looking at the Mongols who surrounded her, Munira could believe all the stories she had heard of them, of how they greased their siege engines with fat made by boiling human captives, and how in their units of ten, if one man hesitated or ran away the whole of the remainder would be executed, even while the battle was continuing; they were more like devils than men and Boru was no better than the rest. Still, she did not want Boru to leave her.

Boru, on this hot August day, was quite unaware of what Munira was thinking and would not have been particularly

interested if he had known. His *arban* (troop) had been practising this morning as usual and it was no different from any other
day. Yet somehow an ancient instinct told him that there was
movement in the air.

Suddenly the order came: 'March'. Boru was one of the first
to receive the command for he belonged to the forward skirmishers. All they needed to do was to ride back to their huts or
tents, collect all their meagre belongings and set out. As they
probed ahead, sometimes fanning outwards, sometimes criss-
crossing, sometimes even galloping back with messages, the rest
of the army fell into line and followed. Then came the *mingans*,
each of a thousand men who were all shock troops. There
was great rivalry between skirmishers like Boru, and the
mingans; both thought they were the pick of the army, and
both had an undisguised contempt for the non-specialist
soldiers, and even more for the men with the catapults and
siege engines. Sometimes when the forward troops had failed
to break into a fortification and the siege men had to be
brought up, the taunts from one branch to the other led to
bloodshed.

Where they were going and whether they would fight or not
today Boru did not know. When he was younger he had taken
part in those great sweeps across the countryside in which the
Mongols had covered fifty miles in a day. But that was before
they met fortresses and rough ground. As they began to gallop
off the training ground and back to the camp he remembered
those days in a passing moment. It made him angry. Warfare is
not the same, he thought. Then it depended on you and the
speed of your horse; now it is trickery and heavy equipment.
He despised and hated the experts in this new form of warfare.
In the past they would have all been killed off as being useless
but now they seemed to have become the most important part
of the army. *They* thought so and others appeared to share their
views. Boru did not; he wanted to get back to the open country
where fighting could be done properly.

Within a few minutes he was at the camp. Munira looked up

from rope-plaiting, surprised to see him. 'Why are you here?' she asked.

He ignored the question. 'Bring all my equipment,' he commanded. The other men pushed past her into the hut for they still all lived together in it.

She felt confused and dazed. 'Where are you going?' she asked; and then, feeling that all questions were hopeless, pleaded: 'Will you take me?'

Boru looked at her. For a moment he felt surprised; he had never thought of her away from here, or even that she would want to go. 'Take you?' He nodded his head vigorously, which meant no. Tears suddenly welled up in her eyes. He looked at her, not seeing her as anything forlorn or pathetic, but like a well or a fruit tree which gave comfort or sustenance. 'But I might return,' he added unexpectedly, even to himself.

No more was said. His equipment was hung around him in seconds, the arban formed up, and with a shrill little cry of command they had galloped away. Munira stood watching them, gripped with fear. Behind was the deserted hut in which a few weeks ago she was living with her family. Now they were dead and she, she had no doubt, was with child. What would become of her? It did not really seem likely to her that Boru would ever return. As she watched the clouds of dust gather and billow over the army she felt perhaps it would be as well. But where to find a husband now that the Mongols had slaughtered most of the men in the district.

Out in the front Boru's skirmishers were now moving quickly and easily, happy to be on the move again. There was no opposition. This part of the countryside was already known to them from forays around their camp; as they moved farther ahead it became more rugged and it was not so easy to see what other parts of the army were doing, but they pressed rapidly and relentlessly on. Boru guessed that word had come that the Turks were assembling an army to meet them, or perhaps preparing fortifications. Whenever the Mongols moved they did it unexpectedly. Always their aim was to deceive the enemy. Now he could see by the sun that they were moving north. He was not surprised, therefore, when soon after midday they were given different orders and the whole army swung to the west. During the morning the skirmishers had been ordered to do reconnaissance only, and if they saw any Turks they were not to capture or kill them but let them ride off. They had halted at midday for an unusually long period. Boru guessed that this was to let the Turkish scouts pass back the news that the Mongols were attacking to the north. During the midday halt they were told not to let any more Turks escape. Boru was well aware of what they were doing: they were deceiving the enemy by sudden switches of line. It was a technique which had been invented by the great Genghiz Khan, a past master of subtlety and intrigue and he did it with tens of thousands when others could only do it with hundreds.

In the late afternoon they halted again, refreshed themselves by a small lake, and changed horses. The order now came that they should put on their silk shirts. These, which fitted closely to the skin, were only worn in battle or when battle seemed likely; they were too hot for travelling. Unlike ordinary silk garments, which were cool and comfortable, these were thick and closely woven and their great advantage was that if a man was hit by an arrow the point would not lodge in the skin but could be withdrawn; they could also turn some sword cuts. While they were here, to his surprise, Boru saw one of the *toumen* commanders (a toumen was 10,000), a man of high rank, give orders for his tents to be set up. Boru then knew they must be expecting fighting very soon for this was clearly a battle camp. These tents were of the conventional Mongol pattern, unlike some of the accommodation they had been using recently. They were made of felt stretched over a light wood framework, circular in form; the felt had been whitened with ground bone ash which made the tents cooler in the sun; in other regions the felt would be soaked in grease to make them warmer.

This was a short halt. As they moved on Boru felt weary and sluggish; he knew it would pass quickly and it did. Soon they were moving swiftly again, more alert than ever.

Suddenly they saw the enemy. There on the plain ahead was a vast army of Turks. It stretched back to the horizon and seemed to be full of twinkling points of light. Those flashes of course would be reflection from armour or swords, Boru knew well, but for the moment it seemed as if he was looking at a lake with waves rippling in the sunlight. It was a shock, for the Mongols did not usually allow others to surprise them: they themselves were the masters of such tactics. Already the signaller in his troop was flagging the message back to the rest of the army. Boru noticed that others were doing likewise. Almost at once he heard the drums and trumpets begin; in the same moment he felt his horse give a little surge. When it happened – as it always did – he always thought for a second of how strange it was that the horses enjoyed a battle, that they too would join in, kicking and biting when they got the chance, yet they were the greatest sufferers. One of the most irritating features of a battle was the screams of wounded horses, particularly from the first flight of arrows when such distraction was especially unwelcome.

All this was merged into one single piece. Instinctively, and without realizing it, the troop were moving diagonally across the enemy front. Now that they had been checked they had picked up their formation – they had practised this so often in training and even in other battles. As they thundered up to the Turks who were prepared, but not fully ready to receive them, they launched a continuous stream of arrows. Seven hundred years later different antagonists would fight to the death over the same ground and their rockets and missiles would look much the same; indeed the tactics would be much the same. As Boru's men galloped off to the right flank he knew that the other skirmishers had moved off at equal speed to the left. The arrows had done some hurt, mainly to the horses, but many of the Turks were wearing chain-mail or padded jerkins, both of which they captured or copied from the crusaders, and the Mongol arrows did too little damage.

Boru saw none of this. He was now in a wide circling movement designed, if his horse could stand it, to surround the Turkish lines. Behind from the middle of the *harb* (army) he knew that there would now be another great pincer launching itself and the enemy would not easily know which claws were closing on them. As Boru's troop galloped wide and clear of the Turkish army the main Mongol formations, preceded by the toumens, came in at the 'wolf lope', that steady pace which was no good for reconnaissance or skirmishing but which when used by thousands was like a great stone rolling forward. The first lines of Mongols took fearful punishment. They were pushed forward by their own advancing army and pinned against the Turks who had chosen this ground to fight on and meant to hold it. Both armies were used to carnage but this moment shocked all those who survived. In later years they spoke of it in the tones in which men speak of events that only the participants can understand; they mean nothing to anyone else.

But the Mongol advance had made a dent in the Turkish front. It was done partly by killing and partly by their technique of pulling men off their horses with the hooks on the backs of their axes. It was not too difficult to parry a blow but almost impossible to avoid being dragged off one's horse by the long hook, particularly as the Mongol holding it was out of reach of a sword blow. Boru was not concerned with this, although he was as expert as anyone else in the technique: he was galloping clear of the Turks in a very wide sweep. Once clear they halted and regrouped; this gave the horses a chance to recover and for the arban to collect fresh arrows. But time must not be wasted; the noise of battle, although some distance away, was audible. That alone, if discipline had not sufficed, would have spurred men on.

The aim now was to break up and destroy the flanks. Later the rear would be put to slaughter but by then the battle would be won and there was no joy in killing the rearguard; it was an exercise in swordplay, no more. Sometimes there was a pocket of resistance which killed a few Mongols but for the most part men, women and even children waited with staring eyes for their fate. They hoped to be spared but unless the Mongols particularly needed a labour force they would be killed. It was senseless but it was the custom. Out in the Far East Mongol armies had obtained valuable recruits from conquered armies but it was not the custom here; Sabutai, the great Genghiz's nephew, was too scared to take such risks. Although great in rank he was a little man and the army had no faith in a man who could never show mercy.

Now they were moving again. Boru's arban was on the left of the line and as they closed on the Turkish flank he was one of the first into action. He had loosed off three arrows directly ahead as he rode in but although each found a target there were many more Turks waiting. He clashed with a small man first. The Turk looked easy but he twisted and turned. When they had aimed blows at each other, the man was caught by an arrow which pierced his face. Boru did not pause to finish him off. Already the trumpets were sounding. He wheeled and moved away.

Every Mongol knew that this was a ruse but the Turks were completely deceived, broke their formation and followed. Boru's arban, now down to six men, rode away sideways, luring out the enemy. At the moment when the whole Turkish flank was in disarray the second pincer rode past Boru and into the battle.

Now the killing was at its height. Waiting for orders, Boru rode up to a little hillock and watched. Even with the success of their tactics all was not going too well for the Mongols. There seemed to be large numbers of well-armed Turks who were still not committed to battle; the Mongols could not lose, but it was taking time.

Suddenly Boru's scowl deepened. The toumen, which included some of the unconquerable Kershih, the crack troops of the Khan's guard, were being driven back. This was no feigned retreat; this was defeat. Boru looked around for orders. There were none. Glancing to the right and left he realized that the sharpshooters had lost their central command; some were waiting, others were slowly moving towards the battle.

Boru was no great strategist, nor even a tactician, but he was a *noyan*, a commander. A noyan might command ten men or ten thousand: Boru commanded ten; there was no one else to give orders so he gave them. Turning to his trumpeter he said: 'Sound the final charge'. As the high, grating notes of the trumpet reverberated through his ears, Boru, his arban, and a few hundred others, were on the move. As the Kershih fell back, dying when they could, but it is not always possible to die in battle – sometimes one is forced to one side even as one longs to kill – Boru rode through the gap. The Turks were bigger, better armed and less disturbed than the Mongols. Boru caught his first man through the throat, aimed a slash at a second and then was tossed forward by colliding horses. In a second he was on the ground. He was not alone; other men, Mongols and Turks, had lost their horses. He plunged forward to the nearest Turk, half tripping over a body. The man threw up a shield and aimed a counter blow. Boru laughed and prepared to drive his sword home as the man, off balance, swung past him, exposing his neck. Boru did not even see the lance which a Turk drove precisely into his left side, slicing the silk shirt as it went.

Back in the village Munira watched the remnants of the defeated Mongol army return and regroup. When men tried to seize her she said: 'No, I belong to Boru, the noyan.' They did not know Boru, but the word noyan means any commander and they were afraid that Boru might be very powerful.

But the Mongol tide had nearly reached its farthest point. Soon their army in Palestine was defeated again by Kutuz, the great Mameluke general. Gradually they were driven out of Palestine and Syria although they held on to their other conquests.

These were hard times for Munira but she had two great

assets: she was very beautiful and she rarely made the same mistake twice. Long before her son was born she had become the wife of a Turk; when the boy was fifteen she had become the wife of a merchant who lived on the coast near Gaza. The boy was fascinated by the sea and at the first chance joined a trading ship which probed around the Mediterranean. It was the first of many ships which he sailed and when he was thirty-two he had his own boat with comfortable accommodation aboard for his wife and two children. He was becoming very prosperous when a sudden storm in the Adriatic wrecked the boat. He, his wife, their eldest child and all the crew were drowned but his youngest child, who was too young to be on deck, survived. In spite of the tremendous battering the boat did not sink and the hulk was driven ashore, where the child was found, hungry, terrified, but unhurt. The fishermen who were first on the scene felt it was a miracle, like the story of the infant Moses. They took her in and brought her up in a family in Ancona. Like her grandmother she was very beautiful and clever so when she was only fifteen she made a very good marriage. Her first son was neither beautiful nor clever; he bore a close resemblance to his grandfather. As a boy he was teased and called 'the Chinaman'. In consequence he was often fighting and felt a stranger even in his own family, but he never made the same mistake twice either.

PIETRO

The Italian Medieval Mercenary

1326 was a quiet year in Italy. Every year since 1321, when he had joined the mercenaries as a lad of sixteen, he had always been told: 'It's quiet this year but there's a lot of fighting going on and one day it will be our turn. You might not be as pleased as you think when it happens.'

Pietro had heard it all without paying much attention. He was already aware that many of the company, even the junior commanders, were slightly afraid of him. He regarded the fact with mixed feelings: it was good to know that men respected you and were wary of offending you, but he was not too happy about his occasional wild rages when he acted in a way he could hardly believe afterwards. The officer had said: 'You need to learn to control yourself, Pietro. A soldier who goes into a blind rage is no good to anyone. He gets isolated and he gets killed. You must keep with the others.'

Pietro thought about it. Normally he was quite calm, but once on a very hot day Carlotti had said: 'You're not like a human being, Pietro. You never seem to sweat. I reckon there must have been something funny in your family. Maybe your grandmother was a dog or something and slobbered instead of sweating.'

Carlotti was a fool, always talking nonsense, but a good man because he kept everyone cheerful. He made everything, however bad, into a joke. When he had a lot of fleas he said: 'I'm feeding them so that when they are big enough I'll ride them instead of them riding me.' That sort of remark kept people from getting too irritable, yet when Carlotti, whom he liked, had made that remark about him not sweating Pietro had rushed on him, and half killed him before Carlotti had even realized what was happening. Pietro felt he might well have finished him off had the others not dragged him away and held him to the wall at stiletto point. No, that was disturbing. Afterwards the captain had said: 'Don't let it happen again. Don't let it, see. This company is a pretty mixed lot and I don't understand half of them, but if a man is going to start killing his friends he will go. Understand?'

Pietro had nodded. He understood what the captain had said all right but he could not explain the blind rage which had taken him. He did not want to leave the company. If only they would do some fighting perhaps he could get himself promoted; if he was captain they would do plenty of fighting. The captain was very clever and he had hired the company to one state after another. They were beautifully equipped and well-trained but just when they were going to battle they were always halted and learnt that peace-terms had been arranged. They were always paid and they seemed to get more for not fighting than for risking their lives. He knew they could fight all right because several times they had been ambushed – treachery was everywhere – and they had completely turned the tables on the ambushers. Last year when they had been caught in a valley they had swarmed up the sides like monkeys, caught the ambushers who were rolling down stones, and rolled them down instead. But all this was nothing to what they could get if they really went to war; the plunder and the ransom for the prisoners would be worth a fortune. This was a good company, men did not desert or mutiny. In other companies he had heard that pay was often months in arrears. Most of the other soldiers were content to march about the country for first one paymaster and then another, never having a formal battle but being paid just the same. 'Why don't you keep your mouths shut?' they used to say to the ones like Pietro who wanted to get the experience of a real battle. 'Can't you see when you are on to a good thing.' One of the men, Luigi, had been in a battle outside Florence when there had been a lot of English and German mercenaries involved. At the end of the day the field was full of heaps of corpses; Luigi had been wounded and was half-buried by bodies but at the end of the battle he had managed to struggle clear and limp away. He had sworn he would never be a soldier again after that, particularly when he was busy praying under all those bodies, but what else could a man do, he asked? You stood less chance of being killed if you were a soldier than if you weren't.

It was 5 September 1326 and they were all out on muster parade. They had been based on this little town of Lacora for two months and they had lost more men in the time in fights in the stews and taverns than they had lost in the past year. Last night, the captain told them, two more had been murdered. 'If this goes on', he said, 'we shall not have 400 men in the company, we shall be lucky to have four. But it won't', he added sharply.

Pietro liked the captain. He was always calm and seemed to think life was rather a joke. He was an aristocrat, his father was a prince, but he was more enduring than many men in the company. He was a brilliant swordsman; any man who challenged him to a duel was simply condemning himself to death, and he was undoubtedly very clever. It would be interesting to be in battle with him because he would clearly know just how to hit the enemy in the weakest spot. The captain might not last very long because personal danger meant absolutely nothing to him; he would ride wild horses or plunge into flooded streams; there was nothing he would not venture.

'Today', the captain went on, 'we need every man we have. We have no men to waste in fights over women or drink. We are going to battle.'

He paused, letting his words sink in. 'To battle', he repeated.

A tremor went through the company. They were not afraid but they were surprised. Pietro could hardly breathe. This is it, he thought, but where?

'I shall not tell you where you are going', said the captain, 'because bad news travels fast and it will be bad news for our enemies. And I want them to receive all the bad news at once, when they see us, and not before.'

There was complete silence. It was uncanny; normally when the company was given information or admonished on the parade ground there would be little murmurs and the senior *condottiere* would have to tell men to keep quiet. On those occasions the captain did not seem to mind if they made a noise or not, he just stood looking at them without showing any particular interest. Now, seeing how transfixed they were he smiled slightly. 'We are', he went on, 'a light infantry company. Every man here can use a sword and bow and can move fast on his own feet. Some of you are getting fat and you all drink too much, but when we get on the move we'll soon put that right.'

A little murmur went through the company. It was a humorous remark but the joke was against them; their chuckle sounded more like a snort. The captain, of course, did not care whether they thought it funny or not. He went on, now using more staccato tones.

'In a few days we shall join up with a cavalry company and an artillery company.' There was a slight murmur of disapproval at this, and Pietro noticed that the captain threw back his head slightly and continued with icy contempt. 'We shall do this because it is in accord with the *condotta* (contract) I have just signed. By its terms, you will be interested to know, each soldier will receive four florins a month.'

Four florins a month! They had been getting three. This was high pay indeed; a man could buy all the drink, meat and clothes he wanted with four florins a month and still have money left over. But what were the conditions?

'Two hundred of you will remain as infantry, and your task, as usual, will be the hand-to-hand fighting. These will be Ranulfo's squadrons.'

The designated infantry broke into a chatter of approval but it quickly died away.

'Florio's squadrons will become shield and lance men. Their task will be to protect the cavalry company from attack, and to follow them into battle when they charge.

'The other company will consist of crossbowmen and siege-craft men. They will learn to be specialists. Their commander, Lorio, was fool enough to get himself killed last night. Pietro will take his place.'

Pietro had never been more astonished in his life. The captain must be having one of his little jokes. He had worked catapults and he was as good with the crossbow as any of them, but he had never taken part in the storming of a city, as some men had; still the captain had spoken.

As Pietro recovered from his surprise he saw the captain had turned and was beckoning some men to bring forward a hand-cart. As it drew level the captain called out, 'Come forward, Pietro.'

Still dazed, but quick and alert, Pietro moved forward. The captain looked at him quickly, then turned and whipped the covering off the handcart. There, as far as Pietro could see, were three iron tubes each with a bulge at the end, and three forked sticks.

'Well', said the captain, 'do you know what these are?'

Pietro peered at them closely, then straightened up and shook his head. 'No, captain. What are they?'

'They are fire-guns. You will learn to use them, and you will train the others to use them. They are the very latest invention in weapons. Nobody else has them.' He grinned. 'They will make us the most feared company in Italy. Look, we will show you.'

He turned to the men who had brought up the cart. 'Show them,' he ordered.

Carefully and slowly the three men who had brought up the cart each took out one of the forked sticks. At the opposite end the stick was pointed and with some difficulty they began to force the points into the ground. Two of them were eventually forced in far enough to enable them to stand upright but the third suddenly broke leaving a sharp point which gashed the man's hand deeply. He gave a yelp of pain and held it with the other to staunch the blood. The captain looked at him coldly. 'That's a good start,' he said. 'All right, help the others.'

The man, white-faced and in some pain, fluttered around ineffectually. There was nothing for him to do and he knew it. After a moment the captain forgot he was there and he spent his time trying to check the flow from his bleeding hand.

The other two now took the tubes from the cart, an iron bolt, which looked like a crossbow quarrel, a small bag, and a match. Pietro looked at them closely. He had once seen 'Greek fire' used: it was a mixture of naptha, oil and ointment and only the men who made it knew the closely-guarded secret; this was clearly something like it; however, it was not exactly the same. He watched closely, fascinated.

Still slowly and even more carefully the fire-gun men put the bolt (which was longer than a crossbow bolt, he now noticed) into the tube. Next they put the tube so that one end was resting on the forked stick. Then from the little bag they poured a black powder into a hole on the upper side of the bulge. Some of it spilt on the ground and some blew away as they poured but a lot of it went through the hole. Still deeply interested, Pietro wondered what this process would be like if enemy arrows were thudding around and the noise of attacking infantry was getting closer. When the powder was in, one man took flint and steel and lighted a long match. He turned in triumph to the captain. 'Now,' he said.

Almost as he spoke they brought the lighted match up to the powder holes. One went out immediately, the other ignited with a roar sending a cloud of black smoke into the air and the bolt about ten feet out of the tube. The forked stick fell over. The captain bit his lip and looked annoyed.

'Do it again,' he said.

And they did; they did it again and again until all the powder was finished. The men standing in the company ranks could not see exactly what was happening but they received the impression that all was not going exactly to plan. By the time the powder was finished the captain had lost his normal composed look, the fire-gun men looked hot, perplexed and slightly frightened, and Pietro wondered whether this extraordinary scene could really be true or whether he was dreaming it all. But if he had been asleep he would certainly have been awakened by the sharpness of the captain's tone.

'You fools,' he said to the fire-gun men. 'Why does it not work? I will have you garrotted.'

'We do not know, captain,' they pleaded. 'Perhaps the

powder was damp. It is a new weapon. There are bound to be mistakes.' They rambled on. Pietro noticed that they called their guns *vasi* (jars).

The captain pulled his lips back from his teeth. 'There will be no mistakes. If it does not work at the same time to-morrow . . .' he said. 'It worked in Florence. If you wish to see your wives and children again it will work here tomorrow.' He hissed the last words with such menace that even Pietro felt a slight qualm. Then he turned irritably to his second-in-command. 'Dismiss the company', he said, 'till tomorrow.'

And that might have been that, and a good day for Pietro. But it was not to be.

The muster ground was on a flat piece of earth just north of the town. There were some tents near by but most of the men were now living in houses in the town itself. As Pietro walked back he thought what fools the fire-gunners had been not to realize that a parade ground would be beaten hard by men and horses. No wonder the forked sticks did not go in easily.

They went through the town gate in small groups, not talking much as it was a puzzling day. Pietro and Carlotti were walking together when suddenly their attention was caught by shouts and screams. In the street on the right of the gate a house was on fire; it was a three-storey wooden house like most in the town. They drifted towards it out of curiosity. There was a small crowd outside, some of them doubtless from the adjoining houses. Already men were chopping away at the woodwork which ran to the neighbouring houses and other men were drenching the nearest buildings with water. These fires often happened and everyone knew what to do. It was hopeless to save the burning house, but by isolating it you prevented the fire from spreading. It was no business of the soldiers and only idle curiosity brought them along to look.

As they stood there for a moment, half-turning to go, there was a scream from a woman in the crowd. 'My Angelo', she called. 'Angelo, Angelo!' Pietro followed her pointing arm.

There on the second-floor window, with smoke behind, stood a child.

'Angelo, jump!' she cried, but of course Angelo did not jump. He probably did not hear and, in any event, if he had jumped he would have been smashed to pieces on the cobbled street.

Pietro looked at her. 'Fool', he thought, then turned his eyes back to the child. Why the little wretch was imprisoned up there was impossible to guess and was certainly no concern of his, yet, strange to say, Pietro liked children – all children. One day when he settled down after the wars he would like to have a lot of children of his own.

Before he realized what he was doing, he was through the doorway and into the burning building. He was only having a look; this part of the house had a stone floor and stair and he guessed that the woman had been cooking, had knocked over some oil, and now the house was ablaze. It was what usually happened. The flames had run up to the woodwork above. If people kept calm most of these fires could be put out before they became dangerous but people did not keep calm when flames shot up around them, they panicked. This was obviously what this woman had done, forgetting there was a child upstairs. Mostly children were outside; perhaps this one had been ill or had come inside from the heat. It was no concern of his.

The next floor was hot and very dangerous. There was more fire than smoke so it would not be long before it collapsed and crashed to the ground. In the corner was a ladder to the next storey. Smoke was being funnelled up it so he took a breath of the hot air and rapidly climbed, stumbling as he went, his lungs nearly bursting. The next floor was full of smoke and at first he could not get his bearings and see the window. Then, rather muzzily because each breath was painful, making him choke and gasp, he staggered over to it. Here the air was a little better, but not much, as the smoke was finding an outlet here. He grasped the child, who was now scarcely conscious. Down below he heard shouts but could not see people or know what they meant. Grasping his burden he staggered back across the room, found the ladder after a moment, wondered if he was too weak to go on but managed, coughing and spluttering, to half fall and half crawl down it. When he saw the room below, now well ablaze, he felt it was the end. His eyes were streaming and he could hardly see, but, half holding, half dragging the child, somehow he found the stone staircase. Then without quite knowing how, he was in the street.

He did not faint but for a few minutes the people round him were only shapes. First he recognized Carlotti. 'You're a fool', said Carlotti, 'but a brave one! Here, take some of this.' He pushed a flask of wine to Pietro's lips. Pietro gulped it down. Somebody had thrown some water over him to stop his scorched clothes from smouldering. He looked and felt a sorry sight. As his senses came back he looked around for the child. It had disappeared. Suddenly he realized that Carlotti had ceased to support him and someone else was speaking to him. With a shock he realized it was the captain. Gradually his eyes concentrated on the captain's face and what he was saying. It took him a few moments to understand.

'Did you go into that building to rescue that brat?' asked the captain. Clearly he had repeated the question several times before Pietro had understood it and he was even angrier each time.

Pietro, his head still buzzing, nodded. 'Yes, captain.'

'You fool,' shouted the captain. 'You are a trained *condottieri* soldier. You earn *four* florins a day. Only this morning I have promoted you to be in charge of our new weapon. And you risk your life – which *I* own as you are contracted to me – to save this useless brat. Everywhere the company goes we leave a litter of bastard brats, each one potentially better than this merchant's spawn. You, the new flame-gunner, risk your life for this scum. Did you think about the guns?'

Pietro stared back. He saw the teeth, the snarl, the trim beard, and he hated them all.

'For what good they are', he said, 'I'd be better in the ranks.'

He should have known better. The captain did not take a second to make up his mind.

'And so you shall be,' he said. 'From now Carlotti shall take your place.' He swung on his heel and was gone.

The crowd, which had fallen back when the captain was there, now closed in again. Pietro did not see them. All he saw was Carlotti, who looked as surprised as he was and intensely miserable. Suddenly Pietro saw the funny side of it or thought he did. 'Hell and damnation,' he said. 'Good luck to you,' and he put out his hand.

Carlotti, till that moment bewildered and frightened, suddenly broke into a smile. 'Come and drink,' he said. 'Let's go to the tavern.'

'Yes,' said Pietro. 'To the tavern. And let the toast be God rot, blast, damn, curse, and blight all captains and their relations and heirs! We'll drink to that.'

And drink to it they did: they drank through the afternoon, the evening and the night. Sometimes one fell asleep, sometimes both, but nobody tried to rob them: drunk or asleep they looked exceedingly dangerous. Through the night at intervals, the streets reverberated with the cry, 'God rot, curse and blight all captains and princes.' The tavern-keepers were afraid someone would hear and there would be trouble, but no one did. Sometimes they sat and talked quite seriously about themselves, the company and the future. Once Pietro said suddenly, 'Do you know, Carlotti, last night I dreamt about what happened today.'

Carlotti gazed at him in a fuddled way. 'About the guns?' he said.

'No, the fire. Last night I dreamt I was in a fire, somewhere else. It was a sort of fort. It wasn't Italy, it was somewhere by a river; it was too green for Italy. I got out of that fire too, but as I came out I knew that fate was going to be against me. I felt it was unjust. I'd forgotten till now. What do you make of that?'

Carlotti rubbed his hand over his face as if to clear his thoughts. 'I don't know,' he said. 'Perhaps it's something that will happen to you.'

'But it has', said Pietro, 'in a different way though.'

Carlotti thought for a while. 'I don't know', he said, 'my father once fell out of a window before I was born and broke both his legs. It nearly killed him. After he'd been drowned my mother told me about it one day. The odd thing was I had never known about it but I never liked leaning out of windows myself. I don't mind mountains but I don't like windows. What do you make of that?'

'Don't know,' grunted Pietro and they both dozed off. The tavern-keeper looked at them, sick of them, and wanting them to go. But they dozed and drank a little longer. Just before dawn they staggered back to their billet supporting each other. Everything they said to each other then seemed enormously funny.

At one point Pietro said, 'Ca-Ca-Carlotti – you remember I didn't like it when you said I didn't sweat?'

'Yes', hiccuped Carlotti, his hand straying to a scar.

'Well I did in that burning house,' said Pietro and he roared with laughter and they both laughed and fell over in the gutter.

They were home by dawn, and snatched an hour or two's sleep before the next muster. But that was next day and the next day is no concern of ours.

The fire-guns (*schiopetti*) never did work: it was a praiseworthy effort to introduce a new weapon but it took another fifty years before they were worth taking to battle. Their inventors and demonstrators were reviled and jeered at when the handguns did not fulfil their promise; the soldiers who saw their traditional skills threatened were particularly hostile. It had always been the same ever since the first men had tried to use a throwing-axe and it would be just the same when the machine-gun, the tank, and the military aircraft were first produced; first they would fail in trials and be laughed at, then, when they were proved, ultra-conservative soldiers would deliberately misuse them or not use them at all.

In 1329 the company was hired to defend the town of Lucca.

Here they were attacked by double their numbers in the Cerruglio company, a mixed force containing many Germans. When the city fell most of his own company, including the captain and his friend Carlotti, had been killed so Pietro took service with the Genoese, who had bought the city from the conquerors. Eventually he settled down and raised a family in the little village of Livorno. It was too quiet for his restless sons who all drifted away from him at an early age. One of them went on a ship to Barcelona where he soon found a wife. Two hundred years later his descendants were one of the oldest and most respected families in the city. Like all sensible families they looked forward to the eldest son inheriting and expanding their business, which was trading round the Mediterranean, but the son was restless and difficult. He upset his parents by telling them they were dull, smug and unambitious; he was the source of much worry to them because they loved him dearly but could not understand him. His name was Tolosa.

TOLOSA

The Spanish 'Conquistador'

His full name was Manuel Réal Tolosa but the other soldiers just called him Tolosa. That was the way he wanted it. He should really have been called Réal, which was his father's name, or Manuel, but he decided on Tolosa, which was his mother's name. Nobody asked a lot of silly questions in the army; you would not be in it if you wanted to answer a lot of questions about yourself; your name was what you said it was although sometimes on a muster when a man forgot his adopted name, and it was called out twice, a few soldiers sniggered. 'Munoz,' the sergeant would say. No answer. 'Munoz,' in a sharper voice. '*Ah, si*,' Munoz would say, coming to life. He was always forgetting; others did sometimes. Out here it did not matter but back in Spain a man had to be careful about his curiosity; making a joke about a man missing his own name on parade could cause knives to be drawn for some of the soldiers had committed crimes and slipped off to another part of the country and joined the army. Once you were in the army you were safe unless you made a complete fool of yourself.

Tolosa was no criminal but he was somewhat apart from the rest. There were others like him, of course. Sometimes his fellow soldiers said: 'Why don't you go and talk to the *hidalgos* and let them make you an officer. We'll follow you. You're a better soldier than Captain Fuster. We'll see he gets killed in the next battle. We'll be safer with you.'

Tolosa always shook his head. 'No,' he said. 'I know what I want to do, and it is not to be an officer. Plenty of people do, so let them get on with it.' And he would turn away and that would be the end of the conversation.

It was not quite the truth but near enough. Tolosa no longer knew really what he wanted to do or to be. Years in the army and in this climate had rotted his will to think. When he had left home in Barcelona five years ago he knew the distress it must have caused: he, the favourite son, the idolized heir, had left because he could not stomach the dullness of a secure family business. He had travelled to Valencia, leaving no word, and joined a ship which was leaving for America. Once he was on it he felt relieved because however much pity he felt for his family he could now never go back. Once he had thought that, loaded with Peruvian gold, he would return to Barcelona but he no longer thought it. If they could not understand each other before they would certainly never do so now; if he ever returned – if – he would settle in some other part of Spain, but that would not be for years. Hell though this life was he would not be without it as long as he could walk. It was curious to think that his parents could believe anything except that he had joined the army of his own free will. Well, that was all in the past. Strange that the past would not stay in the past but would sometimes come vividly back into the mind, like today. Curiously enough it often happened when you were tense and waiting, as now.

Events had followed so naturally that now it was easy to forget how difficult your hopes and expectations had once been. When he went aboard that ship at Valencia he had really believed the voyage to the New World would be like sailing round the Mediterranean, although lasting longer. Now, even at this distance in time, it seemed a sort of blurred hell with certain moments when survival seemed neither possible nor even desirable. 'Once I set foot on dry land,' he had vowed, 'I will never leave it again.' Today it looked as if his vow might come true. At the end of any day out here there would be plenty of Spaniards who would never see the sea again whether they wished to or not.

The hopes. He smiled grimly. Everyone knew of the gold and silver which was there for the taking; nobody guessed the hazards on the journey. Some men thought they merely needed to wade ashore and it would be given to them by ignorant and frightened natives; the reality was a little different. The natives had their own civilization, and they were not disposed to give up their possessions easily. And although gold was what every man wanted, there were other dreams which men sought to have fulfilled. There was the famed Fountain of Health, some-where deep in the forest, where a man could not only have his body restored but could take a step towards immortality. A company of sick men had been made up to march to it under a native guide; somewhere along some lonely path no doubt their bodies lay rotting and their weapons rusting. It was not the people who defended the treasure of the Andes so effectively, it was their cursed climate. Where else in the world but in this God-forsaken country could you be scorched to a husk by the sun while all the while seeing in the distance mountains with their tops perpetually covered in snow? But the true defenders of this land were the diseases which drifted in mists from the swamps, and the insects which tormented men till they scratched their own skins into festering sores. Even now, in his own company, there was a man with his flesh eaten down to the ankle bone by a great festering ulcer, and the man would go on, driving himself to hobble along till his very bones fell apart. All he could think and talk of was gold, for what good that would ever do him.

Suddenly Tolosa's mind jerked back to the present. A shower of javelins had been flung from the thick screen of jungle on each side of the track. The horses, who were the main victims, plunged, kicked and screamed. Tolosa's horse reared and shied and he had difficulty in pulling it clear of the horse in front which, lightly though no doubt painfully wounded, was rearing and bucking. He looked at the trees. Without thinking, each Spaniard whose horse was still under control had taken up his arquebus and was levelling it towards the dense matting of foliage, but nobody fired; there was nothing but leaves to fire at and they would not be so foolish as to plunge in after their attackers. The Spaniards had learnt their lessons hard but they had learnt them. In their early days in Peru they would have dismounted and plunged into the jungle where they would be torn with great spiked thorns, exhausted by having to hack their way through tangled lianas, and bamboo sometimes with trunks as thick as a man's thigh; in some places storms had blown trees over and piled them into an impenetrable barrier. At the end of it not a Peruvian would be seen, let alone killed, but as they re-formed on the path another shower of javelins would fall mysteriously amongst them. Now all you did was keep your arquebus ready for a glimpse of a brown body and plod on.

This, of course, was the final chance. There were sixty of them here, few enough but probably sufficient once they came to the end of the track. Three weeks ago one of the men had been told by a native woman that there was a great temple in this valley and it was packed with gold and precious stones from floor to roof. There was no reason not to believe her. Everyone of the *conquistadores* knew of the fabulous wealth which Pizarro had found in Cuzco. There were huge vases and statues of pure gold, there were women's dresses made entirely of gold beads, there were bars of silver twenty feet long and a foot wide. Every cavalryman got 6,000 gold *pesos* as his share, every infantryman 3,000; some soon lost their share in a single night's gambling, others were stabbed because they were too lucky, but it was something to have it, even for a moment.

Gold was more plentiful than goods, a pair of shoes cost forty *pesos* and a sword fifty. There was no doubt that the gold and the climate drove men mad. Soon not only soldiers were quarrelling in Peru but even the mighty generals like Pizarro and Alvarado. Well, it would be different here. There were madmen in this company also but Orgonez, their leader, was a man of vast coolness and experience. If anyone could lead them to victory and riches and safe back again it was him.

It was impossible to take proper military precautions. In places the track widened into a clearing and the leading files halted to allow the rear to catch up; then they would move on again but in places the track became so narrow they had to resort to single file. They were not attacked again that morning but the fact that they had been attacked once was a clear enough indication that there was more trouble ahead. Everything depended on how many Peruvians were the guardians of the temple. According to the woman there were only a few priests; Tolosa felt neither sombre nor optimistic; time alone would show – what was the point of thinking about it when nothing you could do would alter it. With sixty experienced cavalrymen they should be a match for anything in this area. But if this was a sacred temple and the Peruvians were going to defend it as such there might be thousands; they would see.

Usually the Spanish broadswords, chain mail, arquebuses and experience gave them the advantage over much greater numbers. True the Peruvians had arrows, javelins, lances and battle axes, but they had nothing to match Toledo steel and they were novices in the art of war. Usually they did not even know enough to post sentries which was why that shower of javelins and that ambush were disconcerting.

Quite unexpectedly the track broadened out into a large clearing containing a native village. It was not surprising that there should be a village somewhere on this track, but it was curious to find that the inhabitants, some twenty or thirty people in seven huts, displayed so little interest in the arrival of the Spaniards. They showed neither fear nor pleasure; they did not attempt to hide their food, nor did they cease to wander about unconcernedly. Tolosa noted that there were very few men in the village, but that could be explained by their being out hunting or by other reasons. All the Spaniards were surprised by this cool reception; Orgonez was heard to say that when the Spaniards had first arrived in Peru most of the natives had been indifferent; in the cities they had a remarkable civilization with streets and temples and elaborate rules; out in the jungle they lived close to the soil, growing their tobacco for snuff and endlessly chewing the *cuca* seeds which seemed to dull their senses against excitement or pain. Orgonez knew what he was talking about; he had been out here a long time. Once he had been with an expedition up into the mountains where it was so cold that he had lost the nails on two of his fingers. He was lucky, he said, others had lost their hands and feet; men ate their horses and the only living creatures which were not hungry up there, he said, were the giant condors.

Tolosa's eyes always wandered to Orgonez's fingers when he

was talking. He thought he himself could stand anything but bitter cold. Every man has his strengths and weaknesses, he knew; Tolosa could stand heat which made other men crumple up and die. It was probably a question of what you were used to: on board ship the soldiers had been terrified but the sailors had seemed to enjoy it; on land the sailors seemed lost without their ship; they even talked about it all the time. It was the same in the army; the cavalrymen hated to fight on foot but the infantryman would fling himself off any horse he happened to be using if there was fighting to be done.

They halted for a while in this village and tried to question the dull-looking peasants, but their efforts had little success. A suggestion that torture might be used was dismissed by Orgonez as being slow and useless. 'What was farther along the track?' the Spaniards asked. The Peruvians did not know; they had never been there, they said. The Spaniards were not inclined to believe them and became annoyed; hands began to stray to sword hilts when they spoke. Orgonez ordered them to remain calm. 'They are probably telling the truth,' he said. 'These people are like animals. They can be useful if they become friendly but it takes a long time to win their confidence.' Tolosa, looking at the dark, wizened countenances, was ready to agree, but he felt uneasy.

Just before they left there was a disturbance. One of the men had noticed an old woman was wearing a jewelled necklace. It was half hidden under her black woollen dress, but he spotted it and reached forward to take it. His name was Montesinos and he was one of those men who can always sniff out something valuable in the least promising surroundings; every unit has someone like him, cursed and envied by his contemporaries. Other men had different skills: Lopez would find food when everyone was starving; of De Soto it was said he could find a bottle of wine on a naked beggar; Sanchez could always find an attractive and obliging woman and men used to say he could find a *puta* (prostitute) in a nunnery.

The commotion annoyed Orgonez and he gave orders to

move on. There was no question of the villagers being friendly now; they were trying to protect the old woman and drive Montesinos away. It was a futile gesture for the Spaniards could have put the lot of them to the sword in a couple of minutes if they had wished. Tolosa was surprised that Orgonez had not given orders for it to be done; most commanders would have done that rather than leave a sullen village in their rear, particularly when they themselves had been ambushed. That these people knew something about it, he did not doubt.

They rode on. The track began to climb and was soft and slippery; in the wet season it was probably a torrent. In the wet season! Mother of God, what those few words meant! Rain, solid sheets of water coming out of the sky accompanied by thunder and lightning which was almost one continuous flicker of light. Sometimes it seemed as if the heavens themselves were splitting with the crash of the thunder as great forks of evil light struck into the earth. In the jungle, falling trees split and crashed as if trampled by a herd of elephants; rivers rose twenty feet in a night, and roared down with tree trunks in their brown swirling waters. When the rain stopped the whole jungle was a swamp, dank and festering with thousands of years of rot and decay, and you could almost see the damp and mildew eat into leather and steel, into men's very minds. Well it was over for a month or two and they could make some progress, although it had left its mark on this track. The dead leaves on it made the surface worse. It was the hottest time of the day, when back in Spain men would be taking a siesta but out here if you stopped to rest you would be eaten alive by insects. But one moment they were toiling up the path, and the next were in open country. It often happened. On the slightly higher land the ground was probably too rocky to support much life. There was, however, another clump of trees ahead.

Orgonez waited till the company was clear of the jungle, looked them over, and set off again. They were proceeding westwards. Early in the journey there had been a few jokes about following the path of the sinking sun, for that was said to lead to *El Dorado* (the Golden City), but jokes and all light-hearted talk had long since drifted off men's lips.

As they approached the grove of trees Orgonez uttered a swift oath and spurred his horse forward. Beyond the trees was a stone building. As they came closer they realized it was a temple, set in a wide hollow which made it invisible till you approached near to the trees; a broad track ran right up to it but there was no sign of a doorway. The temple itself, Tolosa noticed, was built of huge blocks of stone, each fitting so closely to the other that you could not slip a knife-point in between. Men said Cuzco was like it but on a grander scale. How these great blocks were cut and moved by ignorant Peruvians, he could not guess; but here they were, and here for a purpose, he did not doubt.

The track was on raised ground and crossed the hollow. Perhaps these great blocks pivoted and swung open, he thought, if you knew how to work the machinery. On each side of the track there was a broad, dry ditch. Some of the men had already jumped down, prodding with their lances to see if any concealed spikes lay in the undergrowth. It was unlikely, for the Peruvians were better at building than at the ways of war.

Montesinos, inevitably Montesinos, had already ventured a little farther than the others. Having been frustrated over the necklace he was now determined on a bigger prize. A shout of terror, perhaps a cry for help, showed he had found more than he bargained for. All eyes turned towards him. From the undergrowth in front of him had suddenly reared up a deadly *surucucú de fogo*, about nine feet long, Tolosa guessed. Montesinos had his sword in his hand but before he could use it the reddish brown body had launched itself forward. No man's eye could follow the *surucucú*'s movement when it struck. It was the most deadly of all snakes they knew; unlike most snakes it would even approach a camp-fire at night.

Montesinos ran stumbling back, screaming. Other men panicked, shouting, 'Get out quickly, the place is full of them!' Whether it was true or not did not matter, although it could well have been. Then another man shouted, 'Look, in the name of God, look, above us!'

Even in the confusion the shrill terror in the man's voice was clearly heard. They looked. All around the rim of the hollow in which the temple and they themselves stood, were Peruvians. They stood there, motionless, silent, clearly warriors, for many had bows and arrows, though none, he noted, had shields. Even Montesinos's cries died away into groans. There was still hope for Montesinos, although not much, but if the Indians attacked, so outnumbered were the Spaniards that they would all be killed and Montesinos would have plenty of company on his road to purgatory. The snake had struck at his chest but his sword arm had been in the way and taken the poison. The leather jerkin would have prevented the fangs going too deep and now Perez, his friend, was already opening the bite with his dagger point; by this he hoped to squeeze the poison out or let it bleed away. It was too risky to suck it when your lips were as parched and broken as theirs were; the poison could be absorbed through chapped lips and men could die as soon as the wretch they were trying to help.

Orgonez was the first to realize all was not lost. 'Back', he shouted, 'they have not closed the gap. Make no noise but go.'

It was his job to notice such things, that was why he was the leader. As the Spaniards pulled round their horses and clattered up the track the Peruvians watched them silently. Tolosa wondered at what point they had closed in around the hollow – and why they had not attacked. It was a mystery; perhaps the hollow was full of snakes and all the Peruvians needed to do was to keep them there till the snakes took them; but if so, why had they not attacked? Perhaps they had other plans farther down the track on the return journey? Sweltering though it was it did not stop a chill shudder running down Tolosa's spine.

Not a javelin was raised to stop them. They left the clearing and moved briskly down the track. This time the going was downhill and much faster. After a few minutes Orgonez suddenly called out: 'Tolosa, Sinisterra and Lopez; you've got the best horses. Take Montesinos on to that village we found earlier; they've probably got an antidote for that snake bite.'

Terrified though he was Montesinos could still sit on his horse and with two ahead of him and two behind they made fast time.

The village was just as they had left it; a few dirty children still played aimlessly in the dirt, the women were still at their never-ending task of getting the rough food ready for the next meal. Into that peaceful scene the Spaniards burst like a thunderbolt; Tolosa leapt off his horse and ran to the nearest woman. '*Raiz*,' he said. '*Raiz. Surucucú*.' The woman looked at him stupidly and he reinforced his words with a gesture like a snake wriggling and striking. As he spoke and waved his hands he noticed a peculiar delay between his words and her response; it was like shouting into a valley and waiting for the echo. At last she understood and pointed to the hut at the end and without more ado Tolosa ran over to it. Someone was inside; he glanced into the dark interior and repeated his words urgently. An old woman shuffled forward. If this woman was the medicine-dispenser she probably had a quicker grasp than the others; he hoped so. '*Raiz*,' he said. '*Raiz de capitao, surucucú*.' He was not sure whether the words were more Spanish than Peruvian, but he thought they would be understood, and they were. The woman drew back into the hut and emerged again with a paste held in a broad leaf which was folded over and secured by a thorn. This was it; it was a native recipe made from a common enough local plant but it was the difference between life and death. He stepped forward to take it but checked as the woman stopped dead, glaring past him.

He turned. Montesinos, now deathly pale, had hobbled up behind him. This was the woman whose necklace he had snatched; he did not recognize her but she remembered him.

Before Tolosa could prevent her she had dropped the leaf on the floor and ground the paste into the dust with her feet. Then she took a step up to Montesinos and spat slowly and deliberately straight into his face.

Montesinos was by now too poisoned to take much note of what was happening. Already drowsiness was making him droop on the supporting arm of Lopez. Lopez had plunged his sword into the woman almost before she had stepped back. Then he drove it through her twice more as she lay on the ground. As he moved Montesinos slipped from his arm and slowly crumpled into the dust. He gave a long sigh and bent double; the blood from the dying woman welled out and flowed towards him in the dirt. Lucky it was a *surucucú* and not a *jararaca*, thought Tolosa. He would have died just the same, but his death would have been unbelievably painful; he had once seen a man die of a *jararaca* bite and he did not want to see another. All the Spaniards had seen men die of snake bite. There was no need, for the snakes usually tried to avoid you, but the Spaniards were always looking for treasure in dark places and corners and who was to know the Peruvians had not put the snakes there as guardians.

Perhaps it was as well that the rest of the Spaniards rode into the village at that moment. Although there were only a few Peruvians in the place Tolosa had that prickly feeling a man experiences when he suspects there are unseen and unknown watchers.

This time the Spaniards wasted no time halting. Montesinos's horse was quickly taken by a soldier whose own was going lame. At the point they had been ambushed that morning Tolosa felt like an animal being watched into a trap, but nothing happened. With the thought of that vast mass of Peruvians behind there was no thought of delaying or trying to make a counter-ambush; they would not feel safe till they were back in Callao. They did not camp till after dark; it had been a long day.

After three days, in which they travelled from dawn till nightfall, only resting after dark when they knew the Peruvians would not attack, they began to feel safe again. The expedition had been a bitter disappointment; they looked for the woman who had talked of the temple but she was no longer there; clearly a much larger force would have to be organized next time and that meant more people to share the spoil.

But there was yet another blow to fall. Tolosa belonged to Pizarro's army and now Pizarro, finding himself threatened by an envious rival, General Don Pedro de Alvarado, was calling in all his outpost troops; with them went Orgonez, Perez, Sanchez and, of course, Tolosa. By the time that affair was settled the Peruvians, under Manco, the Inca prince, were in widespread rebellion. Tolosa took part in the defence of Cuzco and the appalling withdrawal which followed. Several times he found himself in personal combat with Peruvian warriors whose skill with the lasso made them very dangerous; they could hurl the loop through the air, drop it over the head of a galloping rider and jerk him effortlessly to the ground. So Tolosa never went back to the temple and all he received for his troubles was a wound which ached in the wet weather and less gold than he would have earned if he had stayed at home.

In the last stages he was serving as the escort to baggage trains. Although not yet thirty he was already so full of fevers and aches and pains that his use as a soldier had become very small. With other worn-out veterans he was sent back on a galleon travelling to Cadiz. As the ship approached their home-land soldiers who had talked endlessly about the longing to see Spain again fell strangely silent. They were cut off from the past and could not see a future. In Cadiz many stayed on board, prepared to sail back and forth on hazardous voyages until sunk by a pirate or privateer. Tolosa was more intelligent – and luckier. He soon learnt that there were ships in the harbour taking soldiers for garrison duties in the Netherlands. A year later he was on the garrison of Gravensteen castle, Ghent. He married and lived just long enough to have two children. He was not really happy; nobody really believed his stories of what he had seen in Peru, except a few old soldiers who wanted to tell their own stories and not to listen to his. After a while he scarcely believed his own memory.

Tolosa had been in Peru in the first half of the sixteenth century. The gold and silver of the Aztecs and Incas ruined Spain's economy, although at the time it seemed to be making everyone rich. Tolosa's family gradually became Netherlanders. That was hardly surprising; what was, however, strange was that the great-grandson of this Spanish catholic 'adventurer' became an ardent puritan. In Leyden in 1608 he had met the English settlers later known as the 'Pilgrim Fathers'. They were refugees from James I's England and when they told him of their plans to emigrate to North America he had decided to join them. Two ships, the *Speedwell* and the *Mayflower* set off, but the *Speedwell* sprang a leak and both ships put into Plymouth. The damage was so bad that only half the original party could now go and Tolosa's great-grandson, whose name was Ware, elected to stay behind. 'There will be fighting to be done for liberty and the protestant cause in this country before long', he said, 'and it will need men to do it.'

WARE

The Roundhead Musketeer

Just before dawn on 14 June Edward Ware remembered that it was his birthday and that he was twenty-four. He had had birthdays in strange places since the start of this war but this looked like being the most memorable – if he was lucky. It was hard to realize that today was really his birthday; it seemed a day on which ordinary events would not happen. He remembered his grandfather had always told him: 'Do something important and useful on your birthday. Make it a thanksgiving for the honour and privilege of being able to serve the Lord Jesus Christ, may His enemies be confounded. Amen.'

He was a curious old fellow, his grandfather; he spoke English in a stiff way with a strange accent. Ware had often heard the story of how the old man had nearly gone to America with the early settlers but had landed at Plymouth and stayed there instead. Probably just as well for him he did; he might have had his scalp hanging from an Indian's belt although it would take a good Indian to scalp grandfather. He might be pious but he could be tough and ruthless; he could be cruel too. When he was cruel it was always for someone else's good, or so he thought. Some unpleasant things had happened in this war but by all accounts they were nothing to what happened in the Low Countries when the Protestants fought the Catholics; both sides had blood on their hands there. He could see his grandfather fitting in nicely, bible in one hand and thumbscrew in the other. He wondered what his grandfather had been like when he was twenty-four. He had a rare knack of being able to upset everyone, friends, relations and fellow traders, with his dogmas, but never found himself short of people to talk to. He had said this war would come, and he had almost predicted the year. There had been times when the old man's outspoken views seemed likely to get the whole family into trouble – calling the queen the Papal bride of Antichrist and so on. He had died during the siege of Plymouth.

Well, that was the past. Today should settle the future, one way or the other. The Parliamentarians must win. The captains had gone round the lines the night before telling them that on the morrow they could not lose; they said the Royalists were outnumbered by two to one and were also short of cavalry. Ware only half-believed their story, although later he found it to be true. He assumed it was meant to raise the spirits of those who had never been in battle before. Some of these were volunteers who had joined the New Model Army of their own free will. There were plenty of reasons why a man did that; perhaps he wanted to impress the girls; perhaps he had taken a drink too many in the tavern and boasted within earshot of a recruiting sergeant; perhaps he thought he might get some plunder. Not many people joined at this stage in the war because they were full of religious zeal; that had belonged to 1642 when Ware himself had volunteered. A lot of those idealists had drifted home when the pay fell into arrears; some of them were too old for fighting anyway. Cromwell had called them 'a lot of old decayed servingmen and tapsters', and he was right; but at least they tried. Some of the men here today had been recruited by the press gang; one such company, raised in Kent, had mutinied and been shot down. The captain thought that if he told such men they would have an easy victory and capture lots of valuable Royalist plunder they would fight all right. It was a time-honoured way: you filled the numbskull recruit with ideas about easy victories and jewels to be picked up on the battle-field, and he would give no trouble; by the time he found out his mistake he was in the thick of it and he had to do his best or the enemy would kill him.

This time the captains were probably right; the Royalists were really on the run. The war was by no means over; Leicester had been captured by the cavaliers under Prince Rupert and men said they had slaughtered everyone in the city, but Ware did not believe it. You believed that sort of story when you were a young soldier – thousands had been killed, or a great army of reinforcements was coming to help you, or even that your regiment was to be sacrificed while the rest got away; Ware had heard them all and they were all lies or mere fractions of the truth. But for the most part the army was in good heart today. Sir Thomas Fairfax was as experienced a commander as a soldier could hope for and Oliver Cromwell, who was now second-in-command, had a flair for winning battles. It was astonishing to think that now the Ironsides cavalry was better than the Royalists; if you had prophesied that four years ago, men would have thought you mad.

Well, it was his birthday and provided he lasted it would be the longest he had known. It was not yet light; he guessed it was not more than three hours past midnight. The one thing about war he had never realized was how tired you were most of the time. When you were doing nothing, in winter quarters perhaps, you were tired through boredom. On a day like today you were tired because you seldom stopped marching, and you never had enough sleep. Some clown next to him yesterday had said: 'I thought I might get my head knocked off in this war, I never thought I'd get my feet worn off.' A lot of men had had trouble with their feet, when they had been besieging Oxford a month ago men had bought showy footwear. The best thing to have was a plain buckled shoe, not too light and not too loose, then your feet could swell up but you did not get blisters. Some of the foot soldiers had got themselves long boots, fine for a cavalryman but useless for marching. His own shoes were getting worn. When they left Oxford on 5 June they had been in excellent condition. Since then they had done little but march; nine days foot-slogging can make a lot of difference to a pair of shoes. Perhaps he might pick up a pair on the battlefield today, but it was unlikely; by the time a battle was over he was usually past thinking about shoes. Even if he was not wounded his armour would be dented, his jerkin torn and he would probably be soaked with blood.

It was damp and chilly before dawn. He gave a little shiver and then looked around to see if anyone had seen him; men might think he was afraid. He was, of course, everyone was, but no one wanted to show it, still less be mistaken for shivering with fright when it was only this wretched damp that was eating into you. There were a few people who he really believed never did feel afraid but most were like himself, apprehensive but more scared of showing it to their mates than they were of the enemy. But it was a peculiar feeling to think that a few miles away was an army of thousands of men who would kill you if you did not kill them first. He collected his day's rations from the commissariat cart. It consisted of two small loaves of bread and some boiled beef; it was the best that could be done he supposed, but the beef made you thirsty. They had eaten it on the march and he knew all about its effects. After breakfast came prayers and a psalm; everybody joined in and it made a great throb of sound.

As they formed up ready to march, a cheering piece of news ran through the ranks like wildfire. The forced march yesterday – close on twenty miles – had brought them to within four miles of the Cavalier army. This place was called Guilsborough and the king himself was at Naseby only four miles farther on. Last night cavalry patrols had been skirmishing ahead and had actually captured some cavaliers eating in the Naseby inn. That must have been a surprise for somebody. On this march he had begun to hate the Royalists because they had cleared the country of all supplies as they marched. He knew his own army would have done the same, but it did not stop him resenting them for doing it.

He had already checked his musket and powder. He doubted if he would need his sword; he rarely did. The musketeers always carried swords but seldom used them; that was a job for the cavalry. He preferred it that way. When a man fired his musket to kill it was not so personal as using a sword. Although there were plenty of the Cavalier officers he'd be glad to stick a sword through, he did not feel that way about the rank and file for he had known too many people who had joined the Royalists when he had joined the Parliamentarians; sometimes brothers had joined different sides. It was one thing to fight that sort of a battle with muskets and artillery but putting people to the sword was not to his personal liking. There were plenty who had no scruples though.

Now they were on the move but this time they were proceeding cautiously. Sir Thomas did not want to run on to the enemy unawares and there were plenty of places in this countryside where you could lay a trap for an army. As the morning light strengthened it was possible to see movement on the opposite ridge; somebody who knew the district said it was the East Farndon ridge. Then occurred a long series of those movements that made a man wonder what the commanders thought they were doing. You marched, you halted, parts of the army were wheeled off in a different direction, then some came back. It was just as well the other army was a good distance away for if they had attacked now the Parliamentarians would have been in an impossible tangle, but apparently the Royalists were doing much the same. Ware had never believed all this preliminary manoeuvring was necessary. He had been at Lansdown and Roundway Down and on both those occasions it seemed like a great waste of time to him. What mattered was what happened after the first blow was struck. It was clearly sensible to avoid advancing over wet ground or deploying right in front of the enemy artillery but all this marching backwards and forwards was more like a country dance than a battle. After four hours the Ironsides were still not in battle position and some of the rearguard had been halted so often they had not caught up. From where he was, standing on the ridge, he could see Sir Thomas Fairfax riding down the valley with a small escort. He was surprised the Royalists did not try sending out a strong patrol to capture him but they probably felt it would not work. After a while Ware saw Fairfax's party ride back up the hill; at the same time a similar detachment came from the Royalists' army and also rode down the valley to have a look. So far no one had even fired a shot.

Blakey, the company wit, had said: 'That's Prince Rupert looking for somewhere where he can lose his cavalry.' Rupert's reputation for bold dashes into nowhere was well known and it raised a laugh. Then Rupert surprised them: instead of riding back towards the Royalist army he veered off to the right where he was joined by several other troops of cavalry. The move was seen by the entire front line of the Parliamentarian army, now happy in its position and looking down over the battlefield on which they planned to destroy the Royalists. But Rupert's manoeuvre had clearly upset Sir Thomas Fairfax and the other commanders. Like all cavalrymen they overrated the horse and underrated the foot-soldier. There was muttering in the Ironside ranks: 'Come on, Sir Thomas, don't let it worry you. It's only Rupert trying his tricks.'

But nobody was listening to what *they* said; nobody ever did. Soon a whole lot of orders were being shouted. 'Have a care,' came the cry, warning them to expect the next order. 'Left turn. March.'

That was all very well, but somebody had forgotten they were in battle order, with musket rests, with ammunition wagons and, heaven help us, with pikes. Try turning 14,000 men to the left in a hurry and see what happens. Have you ever had a blow on the head from the side of a pike when a man turns without looking? Ware had and he was glad he was well away from the pikemen today. Some of the shouting and the language from that section did not sound like what you should hear from Puritans. When the army eventually got moving it was more like a great wounded snake than a disciplined body of men. After ten minutes the halt was given and the Ironsides faced to the front. Then came the order to close up; then came another left turn and another march of two hundred paces. If Ware had not been present he would not have believed it; it was more like a clumsy dance every minute. Then some information began to be passed back from the Captain-General. The Royalists were trying to outflank them and make a diversion while the rest of their army escaped. As the message came through everyone at the same time noticed that the Royalist army was also moving sideways like a crab. Ware began to put two and two together. He glanced back towards the bottom of the valley. It was green in the hollow in the middle so there was probably a stream there. The cavalry were not going to risk that. It was all right to send the foot-soldiers up to their necks in black mud but those beautiful horses mustn't get their dainty feet wet. Having upset the whole army by their demands the cavalry would now sit back and wait for someone else to do the fighting. Then at the end of the day they were either first away if things were bad, or first with the plunder if they were good. Ware did not say as much but plenty of others did.

After more short marching and closing the foot-soldiers settled to their battle position. Just in front of the ridge (which subsequently would be known as Red Hill Ridge) was a plateau of flat ground. Here General Skippon, who commanded the foot soldiers, supervised their formation. This took about half an hour but nobody minded much as he was their own general; it was when orders came from cavalry generals who did not understand the first thing about the foot that men resented it. By this time Ware had almost forgotten they had come here to fight. That was the army all over; by the time they'd finished marching you around and messing you about you were glad to get into action where you had only the enemy to deal with.

Someone said it was now close on ten o'clock. Ware did not doubt it, nor did it surprise him. It was what you might expect; you were up and standing-to before 3 a.m. and seven hours later you were still doing a sort of Morris dance a couple of miles away. He yawned as he thought of the extra sleep he might have had – and which he needed – but he did not have much time to think about that. Sir Thomas Fairfax suddenly appeared from the left flank, had a word with General Skippon and rode off to the right. As he went General Skippon called up the colonels and gave them fresh orders; this time they were to withdraw behind the ridge, which now lay at their rear. This was not too difficult; it was better than trying to preserve formation in that sideways manoeuvre. As they came to the top of the ridge they halted for a moment and Ware took a quick glance around him. What he saw gave him a sudden feeling of confidence. On the right he could see General Cromwell pulling back his cavalry so that it rested slightly farther back than they themselves were. There must be something wily in that. On the left flank were the cavalry commanded by General Ireton. They weren't the cream of the Ironsides horse – Cromwell had those – but Ireton knew his job all right. Just before they moved Ware noticed a peculiar manoeuvre in front of Ireton's position; a regiment of dragoons were riding forward on the extreme left and disappearing behind the hedge. He smiled to himself; if Rupert did one of the charges on the right flank he had such a fancy for he would get a surprise there and no mistake. At that point the man behind trod on his heel and he ceased to be interested in cavalry tactics.

Just when Ware had concluded that they might go on deploying all day there was a sudden crash of gunfire. They had not brought many guns but these demi-culverins made plenty of noise. And it meant the battle had started. Soon cannon shot were dropping into their own ranks. Blakey caught it almost at once. Poor Blakey, he had made his last joke. Well that was what war was all about.

Now they were advancing back over the ridge. What caught his eye this time made the blood sing in his ears: right across the middle of the valley was surging a huge mass of Royalist infantry; there seemed to be an enormous number of them. He wondered who it was who had said we outnumbered them two to one; we certainly did not here. The front line was already engaged; he was in the third but it looked as if his turn would come soon enough. The Royalists were better foot-soldiers than he would have believed. How they had come across that valley and up the slope in the time he could not fathom; nor why they had been able to do so. This Ironside army was not a bunch of untrained soldiers; it was the best army in the world and it was being pushed back.

He glanced to the flanks to see if things were better there. Cromwell seemed to be doing very little. Some of his men were charging through the Royalist left but it did not look like the whole cavalry wing; perhaps the rest were going to help here.

It did not look healthy at all; Ireton's cavalry seemed to be doing something but he could not quite see what. Suddenly he caught sight of Rupert. That dragoon ambush had clearly not stopped him though it had probably emptied a few saddles. To his amazement he saw Rupert gallop right through Ireton's wing and disappear. This always happened, it was said; Rupert would carry the line in front of him and then ride miles into the country behind; by the time he got his men together the horses were blown and the battle was decided. That was the difference between him and Cromwell; Old Noll sat tight; he didn't let his horsemen get out of control.

When Ware's eyes came back to the front the scene on the slope had already changed. Somebody shouted: 'General Skippon's wounded.' It was true. Through the gap between the companies came Skippon himself, all the colour gone from his red face, and clutching the left side of his chest. Ware and the whole of his echelon looked at it with dismay, not so much because it boded ill for them but because it seemed such a shame to see the great Skippon feeble and having to be supported on a led horse. 'Never mind, lads,' he said as he passed, 'I'll soon be back.' Nobody believed him but they gave a wavering cheer.

All eyes were now to the front where their own turn was coming soon enough. Someone farther forward shouted: 'Here's fiery Tom, we'll beat them now.' That was heartening – or otherwise. 'Fiery Tom' was Sir Thomas Fairfax himself. It was good to know he was here but any soldier, however critical of his generals, would feel dismay at seeing them in the thick of the battle. It is a general's job to think, not to fight; there are plenty to do the fighting – it's the thinking that's scarce. But even the arrival of Fairfax was overshadowed by the next event. 'Holy Saints,' said the man next to him. 'There's the cavalry and Ireton with them.'

It was the last panoramic view of the battle that Ware had. Ireton's cavalry came thundering in from the left immediately ahead of where Fairfax had just brought the Royalist foot to a standstill. They crashed into the solid body of Royalist infantry still pressing up the hill. It was a mad move. Royalist infantry was likely to be commanded by Astley who had been in this war since Edgehill; they would know how to receive cavalry, and they did. From his viewpoint Ware could see the horses going down; he could not see the pikes but he guessed the cause. He could see Ireton's banner, then that too disappeared. Ireton was down. This was madness.

There was no time to think. Now they themselves were coming to battle. A tremendous surge of energy seemed to race through his veins; in a moment he was full of a savage longing to get at the enemy. No care now of whether he used his sword or not. He got in one shot from his musket and saw a Royalist leap up and fall. There was not time to reload; he flung away the musket and drew his sword.

The Royalists were going down. For a few seconds he was everywhere, leaping, lunging, joining in any fight he could see. This was it, this was the moment. Suddenly in front of him was an open space with only two or three men trying in vain to struggle to their feet. As he looked for an opponent the space suddenly filled. He was surrounded; it was almost impossible to shake clear of one's own side and get at the Royalists. But it was wonderful; this was . . .

That was the last Ware saw of the Battle of Naseby. Several hours later he struggled back to consciousness with the roaring of a waterfall in his ears. There were great weights holding him down and he was gasping for breath; then he opened his eyes.

A feeling of sickness as if he had swallowed something vile made him shudder; a vague shape swayed in front of him. He closed his eyes and felt a fraction better. As his mind became slightly clearer he heard the words: 'This is one of ours. Better help him.'

Forcing his eyes open again was an effort. He wanted to sleep for ever but some instinct told him it would be dangerous to leave hold of his consciousness. He forced his mind to wake up and his eyes to focus; then to his surprise he recognized what he saw.

It was Carter and Lane. What were they doing here? They should be with the baggage train. Scum like that did not come on to the battlefield. Suddenly he felt apprehensive.

'Why it's Ware,' someone said. 'Fancy finding him.' Ware held on to his consciousness with every effort in his body. 'It's Carter and Lane,' he said, trying but failing to smile. 'How are you, boys? Glad to see you.'

There was a pause. 'We thought you were dead,' said Carter. 'We just came to see if we could do anything to help our lads.'

It was a tense moment. 'Good lads,' said Ware. 'I've been wounded I think but not badly. Where's the rest of the lads?'

'Over there,' said Carter. 'Behind the ridge. Think you can manage? We'll see if anyone else of our lads is alive.'

'Yes,' said Ware. 'I'll manage.' He put his hand up to his head which seemed to be bursting. It had a lump on it like an egg but otherwise he seemed all right. 'Thanks, lads, keep looking.' And he stumbled away.

Fortunately the other two were too interested in their self-appointed task to show much interest. Several times he fell over bodies he did not seem to be able to avoid, but he struggled on; anything to put a distance between himself and that carrion pair. Many a time in the past few months he had threatened them for their uselessness with the supplies. Carter was a butcher but the meat he supplied to the army was tough and poor. Ware had long suspected he was a fraud and a thief and his friend Lane was no better. They were obviously robbing the corpses on the battlefield under the guise of helping. He had known only too well they would not be above knifing him in his weakened state. He had not been frightened when the battle was going on, but the thought of being murdered by that foul pair was terrifying.

At long last he reached the camp. It was full of wounded. Some, groaning, were unlikely to live long. 'Have we won?' he asked.

Everyone was so stupefied it took a little time to get an answer. His head ached terribly and it was painful even to listen. We had won. Cromwell had put in a final charge and scattered the enemy but there were thousands of dead on both sides. Everyone who could walk had gone on with the pursuit. There were a lot of harlots in the Royalist train who had all been put to the sword. But there was not much news, or food, or water. The baggage park had been scattered by Rupert who, as usual, had ridden right off the field; the baggage men had mostly escaped by fleeing. Men were grumbling and saying they should have come back to help the wounded. Where could they have got to? men asked. Ware knew, but he kept silent; there was no point in making things worse. If he survived he would see to Carter and Lane, but the time was not yet.

Suddenly he remembered it was his birthday. He was twenty-four and alive. Well tomorrow would be another day, even if it was not his birthday. There was nothing to stay awake for so, finding a piece of smooth ground, he lay down, closed his eyes, and dozed off. He was very tired.

Ware never fully recovered from that blow on the head and Naseby was his last battle; nor did he ever find a satisfactory explanation to what had stunned him. Some said a spent cannonball must have struck him a glancing blow, others thought it must have been someone using his musket as a club, while others thought it might have been a blow with the side of a pike. Neither his eyesight nor his memory were quite the same again though the scenes of the early stages of the battle were firmly printed on his mind. By the end of 1645 he was back at his old trade in Plymouth as a cooper. He soon married and they had a family of seven. The seventh child was a boy called Septimus. He was unlike the other six and was a worry to his parents for he almost lived on the sea, but he never seemed short of money. When Septimus was twenty-six the Customs officers had reason to believe that a good part of his trading profit came from contraband. Not wishing to answer a number of awkward questions Septimus slipped over to St Malo, planning to stay until the matter blew over. Soon he was running an even more profitable trade from St Malo. He already had a wife in England but did not think it necessary to mention the fact to the daughter of the wealthy chandler he married. In the circumstances it did not matter, for soon after his son was born he was killed in a brawl which he had helped to start. The daughter of the wealthy chandler had no hesitation about the next husband she wanted; he was a placid Breton farmer, quite different from the rogue from Plymouth. Septimus's son never learnt a word of English and no one ever told him he was not completely French. He inherited the farm and most of the chandler's money. Over the next hundred years a few members of the family joined the army or the navy but they made no special mark; to be frank they showed little liking for a hard adventurous life and soon went back to the farm. It looked as if the spirit which had driven Norsemen and Romans and *conquistadors* and crusaders had been bred out, but in 1801 a youngster called Jean Varelle reached the age of eighteen. His father wanted him to stay and help him with the farm; his mother adored him and wanted him to stay at home whether he worked or not; Jean loved them both but had not the slightest intention of conforming to the wishes of either. He had always wanted to be a soldier and on his eighteenth birthday he went to the recruiting office in Dinan.

VARELLE

The French Cavalryman of the Napoleonic War

On the morning of 2 December 1805 Varelle was suddenly overwhelmed with a feeling of his own insignificance. It was a feeling which men experienced from time to time in the army, but usually the importance of doing a particular job or even chatting to one's comrades dispelled it at once. Today was different; somehow today he felt himself to be a mere fraction of his former self and the feeling would not leave him.

So far in the army he had felt important. At the beginning, even when he had made mistakes and been laughed at by the older men, he had still felt that one day he would be as good or better soldiers than they were. He was Jean Varelle, son of a prosperous Breton farmer, and one day he might distinguish himself. He was not, he found, as quick on the uptake as some of the men called up from the cities but he knew more about horses than most people. When in 1803 he had been selected to be one of the famed *chasseurs* of the Guard (*Les Chasseurs à Cheval de la Garde Imperiale*), it seemed that all his ambitions were now fulfilled. Other regiments might have given him promotion or an easier time but nobody in his right mind could really wish to be anything but a member of this *corps d'élite*. Every Monday and Thursday they used to parade at 7.30 a.m. on the Champ de Mars on horseback; every Wednesday they did foot drill; on other days they practised swimming and rowing. There were 56 officers and 959 men in the regiment and every one of them was worth two or perhaps three in another regiment. This was no idle boast; although at the time of the Battle of Marengo in June 1800 the chasseurs had only been a company named the *Chasseurs à Cheval* it had fought better than other entire regiments. The cost had been huge; they had lost 70 out of 115 horses but the damage they had inflicted on the enemy had made the Italians catch their breath. He had heard of its famous deeds in those days but had never dreamt he would have the chance of joining it; then the word had been sent around that crack horsemen were needed for this distinguished regiment which was also the Emperor's bodyguard and he had been allowed to volunteer.

He gave a grim little smile as he thought of those far-off days. It was not so much that they were distant in time but that they were so remote in thought. Looking back it seemed as if they had been partly play-acting. It had all been useful training but it was surrounded with the glories of war not its realities. He remembered one of the legions of girls who had flung themselves at the soldiers of the regiment. She had suddenly said: 'You will never come back to me. You will go away and will kill thousands of people whom you do not know, whose countries you do not even know, and there will be many girls' sweethearts, and at the end what will you have done? Will you have made anyone happier when it is all over?'

Well it was a long way from being all over, and then he would see. But the woman had talked sense; with that peculiar mixture of blindness and insight which all women seem to possess she had loved the finery, the trappings, the whole structure of the army, and yet underneath she had known, with a chilly fear, that it meant hunger, fear, loneliness, confusion, and painful death to so many. So many of the victims were innocent, but a soldier must not think of such things. France had the greatest Emperor and the greatest army the world had ever known. They would conquer Austria and Italy, Prussia and Bohemia, Russia and England. Napoleon was the greatest military genius the world had ever known. Nothing would stop him; after Russia and England perhaps India and China would be the next step. By then all countries, even former allies, would bow before the power and glory of France. Damn that stupid woman, she made it all seem so futile. How could she admire his uniform and then say – as she did – she could almost see the bloodstains on it.

It was, of course, the finest uniform in the army. From his black shako with its long green and red fur plume to his black boots with their orange trimmings he was, he knew, the envy of all. His scarlet pelisse (close-fitting jacket), his green dolman (outer loose jacket), his scarlet breeches and his ornamented sabretache (cavalry pouch) made the finest combination of clothing to be found in the whole French army. This was hardly surprising for was not the Emperor Napoleon himself the Colonel of the regiment, often leading it himself on parade and almost always wearing the officers' green undress uniform. Usually the regiment was commanded by a major but he ranked equal with colonels of the line regiments. Most of the men took it for granted that their officers should be men of exceptional quality, Beauharnais, Morland, Dahlmann, Beurman and Hercule. Hercule was in fact a Negro but his military prowess and skill made him one of the finest squadron commanders any regiment could hope to have. Varelle felt irritation rather than pity when he heard soldiers in other regiments complaining about their officers. He did not doubt that the criticisms were justified and it would be infuriating if one of those badly-officered regiments was to fail in its task and hamper the Emperor's plans. Sometimes he felt that men in other regiments deserved little. While they envied the Guard they all swore they would not serve in it for anything in the world. 'Look at you', they said, 'always on parade, always called to turn out at a moment's notice, always cleaning up your kit. Oh, I know you look very smart, and the Emperor takes you into his confidence but you can keep it. Don't you ever let yourself go, relax, take a day off?'

They did not understand and Varelle did not try to explain. There was no point in it.

Although they were jeering when they said the Emperor took his chasseurs into his confidence they were nearer the truth than they knew. Sometimes he would come out of his quarters and walk about for a few minutes; he would stop and talk for a moment to the nearest chasseur, knowing full well that the man would never repeat what was said, and that his comrades, who saw him stop, would never ask. They were extraordinary conversations; you felt that the Emperor had to talk to someone for a minute to clarify his own thoughts. 'Do you know where we are, Chasseur?' he would ask, and before the man could reply he would say: 'We are between Brunn and Ollmutz. We have just retreated from Austerlitz. We have just over 50,000 men and the enemy have nearly twice as many. Our lines of communication are long. If we try to winter in this bleak country we shall starve. What would you do, Chasseur?' The chasseur would think very hard and the Emperor would look at him intensely as if hanging on his answer. 'Well, sir', the chasseur would say, 'I don't quite know.' The Emperor would smile and say, 'Don't you, Chasseur? Well, perhaps that is why you are a chasseur and I am the Emperor.' And he would move on, then go back inside and work out his plans. But the Emperor would listen hard enough if he thought a man had some useful information; he was very fond of talking to local people, asking them what the weather was usually like and how much rain or snow they had.

Well, this time, thought Varelle, he would need all his cunning to bring the campaign to a successful conclusion. Unbelievable though it seemed, the French army was actually on the retreat. They were heavily outnumbered and even if the Emperor pulled up another 20,000 from the communication areas they would still be at a huge disadvantage. Unfortunately the enemy generals, particularly Kutusov of Russia, were experienced and skilful. The Austrians had already shown that they were too rigid and orthodox but that did not mean they could not fight. It was rumoured that the Prussians might join them and that might be the last straw.

Suddenly he came to his senses. What was he, a mere chasseur, doing with such thoughts? The Emperor, who was still sleeping peacefully, had no doubt got it all worked out. All yesterday he had been watching the enemy manoeuvres. This hill on which he was now standing, somewhere near a village called Blasowitz, gave a perfect view of the countryside. It was just the sort of place the Emperor would have chosen; out of a dozen hills he could pick just the one which gave a perfect view of everything he wanted to see. It was clear even to a mere chasseur that the enemy was trying to outflank the French on the right, furthermore it looked as if they would do it. The Emperor seemed actually to be encouraging them; he had withdrawn from Austerlitz and the Pratzen hills and had offered the enemy an almost open road to Vienna. All day yesterday he had watched them manoeuvring into line to do it. At first it seemed as if he might be going to attack the enemy just where the Austrian and Russian forces joined but he made no move, he just watched. In the afternoon he sent for his corps commanders and talked to them; at 8.30 he sent their battle orders to them. Some of these orders were delivered by chasseurs who could hardly guess the details, but in accordance with his custom of letting his army know what the general plan was he had sent out a proclamation which was read to all soldiers. It ran: 'We occupy a formidable position and while the enemy are marching to turn my right they will present their flank to me.' At about 10 p.m. he walked around the bivouacs and was cheered by the soldiers. They made torches of burning straw and waved them and shouted, *Vive 'l'Empereur!'* Then he had taken a small escort of chasseurs, including Varelle, and ridden up to the Satschau to take a last look at the enemy dispositions. By that time it was after midnight; his escort had been dismissed and he had gone to bed; it all seemed so natural and mere routine that Varelle forgot they were probably on the eve of a tremendous battle and went straight to sleep; he was roused half an hour before dawn and was now on picket duty waiting for the next order. Suddenly at this moment he had been swept by that strange feeling of being utterly insignificant; even reminding himself that he was a chasseur did not seem to make any difference. All around him there were thousands of other soldiers; by the end of the day some would be triumphant, some would be groaning in pain and some would be dead. Nobody could possibly know what his fate would be; however brave or skilful you were a chance cannonball could knock your head off; the best swordsman in the world might find himself surrounded by a dozen lesser ones but there could be no doubt of the result. It was this that made him feel so small; it was not a question of being brave for he did not feel at all afraid, it was just so extraordinary to find himself in the middle of such a great mass of people. But it was all over in a flash. The Emperor had suddenly emerged and as if by magic – but in fact by good timing – he was soon surrounded by his marshals. As dawn broke all one could see was thick fog like a great white sea; then gradually hill-tops began to appear like islands. Everybody took breakfast. The Emperor and his marshals were chatting light-heartedly and often laughing; if they were disconcerted by this heavy morning fog they did not show it. As the main part of both armies were in the valleys below this hill they were both invisible. It would be raw and cold down there; there would be a lot of cursing and spitting and falling over stores and tent ropes; it would be a good chance for someone who had lost some kit to lift it from a neighbour when he was not looking. There were rogues in every army and the French certainly had their share of rascals who could never miss the opportunity to steal.

As the mists cleared the whole array came into view and it was possible to see the whole progress of the enemy attempt at outflanking. Much of it seemed smooth enough but even before the French had opened fire there were places where confusion was rampant. Varelle watched, fascinated. Whenever a column tried to cross in the rear of another there was always confusion: whether one column was moving too slowly and the other too quickly could not be determined, although no doubt each was thinking it was the other's fault. Clearly the main weight of the enemy attack was on this side, and it looked as if the French would be hard put to contain it. Generals Legrand and Davout were positioned just behind the stream and as the enemy advanced the French sharpshooters were crumpling up the front rank. It was a remarkable sight, which could probably only be appreciated from a bird's-eye view. The enemy battalion advanced with the leading edge in a straight line, then there

were puffs of smoke from the French lines and the leading edge
of the enemy troops suddenly became jagged; a few minutes
later the edge would straighten but then the whole process
would happen again.

It was quite extraordinary for Varelle to be seeing all this;
it all stemmed from the fact that today was his squadron's turn
to be the Emperor's bodyguard. In the other campaigns they
had been launched into the thick of the fighting at the earliest
moment whereas it looked as if today he would observe the
battle as if he were one of the great marshals. It was an unusual
position for a chasseur to be in but of course like everything
else it must have happened many times before to many different
people on many a different battlefield. Anything can happen in
war.

By now the Emperor's plan had become clear to Varelle.
The enemy column was now strung out in some confusion
between their own position and the Pratzen heights. Now that
the battle had begun the chasseurs were in their appointed
position: twenty-eight chasseurs, including a lieutenant and a
sergeant, were drawn up behind the Emperor and the lieutenant
never took his eye off him. If necessary the lieutenant would
brush on one side anyone except Prince Murat and the Prince
de Neufchâtel. The lieutenant was like a shadow, but never
obtrusive.

Today Varelle was right-hand man in the square. The
square consisted of four chasseurs who screened him wherever
he walked. They carried carbines with long bayonets fixed;
they knew exactly where the Emperor was without looking at
him; their eyes were always outwards and they swept the area
in front of them. One chasseur carried the Emperor's despatch
case, another his field glasses. On a normal day they did two
hours only before being relieved, but today the Emperor
had said they would stay for four as he did not want too
much movement about him when the battle was beginning.
Varelle was delighted. Later, with luck, the chasseurs would
be given their chance in the battle but even if it meant

missing it altogether this unique opportunity of standing by the Emperor at the critical moments was something he would never forget.

At 8.30 the Emperor suddenly addressed a question to Marshal Soult. 'How long would it take you to reach the Pratzen heights?' Soult gave a quick glance below. 'About twenty minutes,' he said. 'Right,' said the Emperor. 'We'll give them another quarter of an hour.'

But it was nine o'clock before Soult got his orders and galloped off down the valley to his troops waiting below. Surprisingly the enemy did not even suspect they were there, but as they emerged there was a tremendous rattle and thunder of the artillery. 'That is General Kutusov, the Russian,' said the Emperor to the lieutenant. 'He is a very clever general. Let us see if he is clever enough to get out of this one.'

As Soult's column carved its way into the enemy flank the French guns seemed to redouble their fury. Kutusov hastily re-formed his marching column and deployed them to meet Soult's attack. Nothing he could do seemed to help him. When he fell back the French gunners hammered him before he was in his new position and when they relaxed Soult's men poured in. Varelle, looking at it from the Olympian heights of the Emperor's vantage point could hardly believe that down there there was a desperate scene of men and horses dying, that there were shouts and screams and cheers and groans. He knew just what it must be like but up here it did not seem that way at all; for a moment he saw it as generals and emperors see it, not as horses and men, and wounds and widows but as numbers and obstacles and mathematical calculations. It would have been interesting to glance at the Emperor's face at this moment and try to see from it what he might be thinking. But of course one would never do such a thing.

At this point he was relieved from special guard duty and took up his position with the rest of the squadron. He was not told whether he would be needed to take a turn on special

guard later or whether, if the squadron were allowed into action
he would be able to go with them. Now he could not see so well
but plenty of information was forthcoming. After two hours
fighting the Russians, although resisting desperately had almost
been cleared from the Pratzen heights. On the other flank,
which lay along the Brunn–Olmutz road the enemy's secondary
attack was being held by Lannes and Murat, although the
latter's troops were really meant to be in reserve. This was
clearly one of the great battles of the world. It had been wonderful to see it but surely it must now be reaching a conclusion
and he looked like missing the active side of it altogether. It
seemed hardly possible, even for the Emperor's special escort,
to be on the greatest battlefield in the world and never strike a
blow.

Another hour passed. It was 12 p.m., time to eat, but nobody
thought of food until someone emerged from the Emperor's
bivouac bringing bread, meat, and water. The Emperor
munched it without taking his eyes off the battle. He was
showing particular interest in the Pratzen heights which by
now should be completely clear. After a few minutes he stopped
eating and handed his food back to the attendant. Then the
news began to filter back. The Russian guard, up till now
uncommitted, had been launched towards the Pratzen heights
and were doing far too well. The Emperor was clearly concerned. He wrote out two messages. 'Take this to Bernadotte',
he said, 'and this to Marmont.' He then turned to the lieutenant. 'You can send six volunteers from here,' he said. 'We
are unlikely to need the full number now.'

The lieutenant turned back to the squadron. 'Does anybody
not wish to go?' he asked cynically. Not a muscle moved.
'Right', he said. 'Fall out the rear ranks and dismiss.' Varelle
was in the rear rank.

From that moment it all seemed a dream. Within minutes
he had transferred from the detached calm of the heights to
the tense urgency of the battlefield itself. The regiment had
been waiting just below the crest of the hill, wondering if its

turn would ever come; now it had happened. They were to be committed at a critical moment in the battle.

As they trotted forward to take their part the chasseurs were left in no doubt of the task ahead. It became impossible to retain exact formation; there were too many dead bodies of men and horses in their path. With the regiment rode the company of Mamelukes who had been attached to them just over a year before. Before they had set off Napoleon's senior A D C had come galloping up to lead the charge. It must have been a setback to Morland but he showed no displeasure.

It was a task which only an élite cavalry regiment could have handled. The ground was obstructed, broken, and often uphill; they were outnumbered; many of Soult's men, wounded or dazed, were straggling back; the enemy, when they reached them, were clearly of the same calibre as themselves. Having virtually regained the heights after a desperate struggle they were in no mood to relinquish them tamely.

In the first few minutes Varelle received a sabre cut on his right arm which made him little more than a passenger. Fortunately he had two pistols in his left holster (he was only supposed to carry one) and with these, with some difficulty he managed to find targets; fortunately for him none of the enemy saw how helpless he was, with a cut ligament in his arm, or he might not have survived. Just when the chasseurs were getting the upper hand they were charged by fresh squadrons of Russians. Afterwards he wondered what it must have all looked like from above and whether it would have been possible to make any sense of it. In the middle it was all heaving, struggling, slashing and trying to stay on one's horse; the gallant Morland was killed by a pistol shot and all the squadron commanders were wounded. When the order came to ride out and reform, Varelle was staggered to see how few their numbers had become. They had, however, captured the commander of the Russian Imperial Guard, Prince Repin, and the French once again controlled the heights. The chasseurs had sustained too many casualties to be used again in the battle and they had the mortification of watching Bernadotte's division drive the remainder of the Russian guard off the field. They were driven on to some frozen lakes where French artillery fire broke up the ice; the scene remained printed on his mind as the most bizarre he had ever seen in all his campaigns.

Even so, the battle was not over till nightfall. By then, as Varelle was waiting to have his wound dressed, it was bitterly cold. As the enemy fled the Emperor came down from the hill and rode over the battlefield. He spoke to each regiment and told them how well they had done. So few were the chasseurs after the battle that Varelle, in spite of his injury, was included in the escort. Afterwards when it was realized how deep his wound had been, he was awarded the cross of the *Couronne de Fer*. Once, as they passed a great heap of French dead, Marshal Soult said: 'We have lost a lot of good Frenchmen here.' The Emperor shrugged his shoulders impatiently. 'They will soon be replaced, a victorious army soon breeds sons.'

Varelle stayed with the regiment till the end, that is until it was disbanded at Périgueux in 1815. By that time he had been wounded three more times and had worked his way up through the ranks to squadron commander. In the bitter disappointment which followed the defeat at Waterloo he felt he could never stay on in France. After 1815 he knew that the Emperor could never return and it seemed as if years would pass before French military power could be revived. The thought of going back to be a farmer in Britanny was ludicrous. There was only one course of action a man could take: over the seas was France's former ally America; by all accounts there was a new world, a new spirit and adventure to be had there, and that is why in July 1817 a battered veteran of the Napoleonic wars set foot on the north American continent resolved to put the past behind him and make a new life at the advanced age of thirty-four.

It was absolutely predictable that two events would occur when this dynamic Frenchman reached the New World. One was that he would soon find a wife and raise a family, the second was that his sons would be as adventurous as their father. There were five of them and they were all surprisingly different. Neither Varelle nor his wife (who was the daughter of a German immigrant), could imagine where all those different characteristics came from. They thought back to their grandparents, which was as far back as either's memory could go, but this threw no light on why one son was tall and fair, another short and stumpy, another rather excitable and yet another the complete opposite; the youngest was the one most like his father. Fortunately they were all steadfastly fond of each other and loyal. However, that did not stop them wandering off in different directions when they grew up. One became a mountain man and eventually settled in Nebraska and raised a family. One of his descendants was the mother of a soldier we come to later, but the one who crossed the border into Canada is our most immediate concern. In the 1890s when numbers of Englishmen were flocking out to see what Canada looked like, this man's son decided to take a look at the country where all those varied immigrants came from. He should have returned on the next ship, but destiny intervened and caused him to meet his future wife; the complication was she did not want to go away at the moment as she was looking after her widowed father. While they were still searching for a suitable housekeeper for the old man, who had a small farm near Oxford, young Verrall (for that was what the name had become) gave a helping hand. He was always 'going back to Canada one day', and his wife was very much looking forward to seeing it, but what with taking on some extra land and the agricultural setbacks at the end of the century, it was never easy to see the way clear. However, in the summer of 1914, with a couple of useful sons to leave in charge of the farm, it looked as if they really might take that long-postponed trip. September 1914 looked a real possibility, when Canada would be looking at her best in the fall. They were both surprised – but not displeased – when Bob joined the army the moment war was declared on 4 August. The sooner they got on with it the sooner it would be over; a farmer at Banbury cattle market had told Mr Verrall it could not last beyond Christmas; the navy would starve the Germans out by then; he had heard it from an authentic source – a friend who knew a Member of Parliament. Still they would miss young Bob at the winter ploughing.

VERRALL

The English Soldier of the First World War

'Bob.'

'What?'

'Do you think the Germans hate us?'

Ever since Verrall had been made a T/A/U Lance Corporal three weeks before, people had been asking him questions. T/A/U designated Temporary Acting Unpaid. The appointment was the creation of some frugal military brain, doubtless long dead. A promising young soldier would be given one stripe, a lot of extra duties, no more pay and no reason to suppose he might not lose this peculiar status at a moment's notice. His former mates resented his minor promotion and often tried to needle him, but that did not stop them expecting him to be the fount of all wisdom and knowledge, the repository for all grievances, and the interpreter of all mysterious orders. Even so, expecting him to read the Teutonic mind was going a bit far.

'How the hell do I know? Makes no difference anyway. If they put a great big kiss on one of those flying coal-boxes it would kill you just the bloody same. What do you care anyway?'

'I don't know really. I thought about it last night when I was filling in that will page in my AB 64.* I thought of my old woman and the kid and mum and dad and how upset they'd all be if I cop it today. I wondered whether the Germans really hated us, like, or whether they were like us, mucked and messed around all day and half the night by their own sergeants and never giving a thought to the enemy, that's us, I suppose.'

'Blimey, you don't half get some thoughts. You remember what they used to tell you in the Depot, "The only good German is a dead one". The sergeant-major was always on about it.'

'Oh him? He'd never seen a German, let alone a dead one. That chap in A Company stores – you know the one that had been in the Sudan and India and that lot – well he said the only time the sergeant-major did any war service was when he was running away from the Boers.'

*AB 64 - Soldier's Pay Book. It had an Active Service will form which did not require a witness.

'Old Smudger, did he tell you that? He's jealous because he's only got one stripe instead of a crown. I'd rather have the sergeant-major here now. That big mouth of his would frighten the Jerries away.'

'I'd rather have the Jerries. He never stopped. "Your mothers won't know you when I've finished with you". "Take that man's name". "Look to your front". "Stand still". I've seen some useless sods in my time but I've never – do you know, Bob, I think I'll never forget that blasted voice.'

Bob glanced sideways quickly. It was 'Taffy' Rees going on. What a thing to be talking about; the company sergeant-major in the depot. Just another of the loud-mouthed brigade they put in the depots to break in the rookies; it was probably all they could do with him. The warrant officers and sergeants out here were much better.

They were standing in the trench, waiting. Here they were, in the trenches after eighteen months waiting about and they were still waiting. It had taken eighteen months, more, twenty months, to get from a recruiting office in Oxford to a trench near Arras; he could have walked the distance there and back a dozen times. But why had it taken so long? Because he'd spent half the bloody war so far waiting. He remembered on his very first day being marched – they were all in civvies and they looked like nothing on earth – to the company stores to draw blankets. There was a notice on the door which said 'Knock and Wait'. They weren't kidding; and wait; and wait; and bloody wait. And now, at long last they were all jacked up to kill the whole German army and what were they doing? Guess, you never will. Waiting. Once in the early days they had all marched to the cookhouse and then been stood easy. 'Wait here,' said the sergeant to the corporal and pushed his way through the doors which were normally open when they arrived. So they waited, but he didn't appear. Dusty Miller said, 'I expect the cooks have flogged all the rations, and he wants his share of the loot.' 'He'll be lucky,' said 'Chota' Harris. Harris was a little tick of a chap so they called him *Chota* which is Hindustani for small.

Nobody had been in India but it was all *dhobi* and *jilo* and that lot. Anyway somebody started singing 'Why are we waiting' and they all took it up. That's all you say, dragging it out a bit like a hymn. Suddenly the sergeant appeared. He was bloody *furious*. All these sergeants and sergeant-majors can turn it on and off, just as it suits them. This one had gone purple with rage. 'Verrall, Miller, Harris, Clegg, Lambert – stop that bloody row – you're on a charge.' 'Blimey, Sarge,' says Clegg. 'I wasn't singing.' 'Don't lie to me,' says the sergeant. 'Orderly room the lot of you at 2 ack emma.' So they waited again at 2 a.m. till half past two when he came out of the sergeants' mess with a skinful – somebody must have been promoted and buying free beer, and said, 'Right, double round the square three times and let's have no more of it. Clegg do it four times for being saucy.' This time old Cleggy kept his trap shut. That was our 'free' afternoon, which meant compulsory games. At three o'clock we were waiting for the referee and at half past four we were waiting for a bath because the whole bloody garrison had got there first!

Who was saying all this? With a start Verrall realized it was running through his own mind. Waiting. If Rees would never forget the sergeant-major's voice he would never – if he lived – forget the hours he had spent waiting.

'Company Atten – shun.'

'Stand at aise.'

'Stand easy.'

'Stand easy.' Well you could call it that, with ninety-six pounds of kit on your back, a rifle that you had to hold anyway and 'DONT MOVE YOUR FEET'. After a while you knew that 'Stand easy' meant wait here for a bit while somebody else wins the flaming war.

He frowned slightly. Taffy looked all right – he hadn't gone barmy with the strain. If only they would do something. The barrage had not completely stopped but only a few shells were going over now. The Boches were pumping plenty of theirs into our rear areas. He wondered why. They would certainly be making a right old mess among the second line reinforcements and the communication trenches. He wondered why they bothered. This was only a small attack, Captain Evelyn had told them. The Germans would be taken by surprise and the battalion would just capture a useful piece of salient and some prisoners. Clegg said, 'I hope the Jerries know. I wouldn't like them to think they'd got to do any fighting. Just let us go over the top and home for dinner.' There was always someone like Clegg wherever you went. He couldn't keep his mouth shut even if it did give him a crime sheet like the *Police Gazette*. But Clegg was a good lad. He was five along the line and Verrall did not doubt that he was talking at the moment. He'd got pretty artful with experience. The sergeant called him 'a proper barrack-room lawyer' but he usually pretended not to hear what Clegg said nowadays. Last week just when the sergeant was passing, Clegg said to Chota: 'Do you know, Chota, I've just heard some wonderful news, the sergeant's mother and father are going to get married.' The sergeant must have heard but he took no notice.

Suddenly the order came to stand down. Clumsily, for they were carrying trenching tools as well as ammunition and kit, they dropped back into the trench. Captain Evelyn, who believed in keeping everyone informed, came along the trench saying: 'There's a slight delay. The attack has been postponed. But don't worry, lads, you'll have your chance in a minute or two.'

Hardly had he gone round the corner when the German shell fell. Bits of Captain Evelyn and a few others fell over Verrall, Edwards and the parapet; they could hardly believe it. 'Blimey,' said Taffy. 'That was quick. Sod the Jerries.'

And still they waited. By now the Germans were paying attention to the British front-line trench. The shell that had killed Captain Evelyn was no isolated shot falling short. 'Here, hang on a minute, Jerry,' came Clegg's voice. 'Our gun's broke.'

There was a small piece of bloody meat just above the fire

step in the trench opposite Verrall. He looked at it and tried not to think this had a short time ago been a part of Captain Evelyn. It was no different from pieces of meat he had often seen in butchers' shops, although perhaps more ragged. He felt he ought to be more concerned about the fact that the cheerful, fussy captain had ceased to exist and that this was a bit of him. Lambert's voice broke in on his reverie. 'The cheeky bastards, killing our officer like that. I thought officers didn't get killed. It don't seem right somehow.'

That moment was a turning point. Verrall stopped looking at the bloody fragment. It did not seem to matter any more.

But they waited. A few more shells dropped but the Germans were not taking it seriously. The person who was taking it seriously was the platoon commander, 2/Lt Brandon. He came along to reassure them. You could almost see a copy of *Instructions to Newly Commissioned Officers* sticking out of his tunic pocket. When he had spoken to them and moved on, Chota summed it all up. 'Wet behind the ears that one is.'

The attack, for some mysterious reason, had been postponed for an hour. The soldiers, who had been standing-to since pre-dawn, thinking they would attack at first light, now began to feel slightly disappointed. Lt Kirby, the quartermaster, came along the trench, passing the occasional quip as he went. 'If you lads are waiting for your dinners', he said, 'you're making a mistake. They're being served in the German lines today.' Kirby had worked his way up from being a boy soldier at fifteen. He was never at a loss for an answer. 'You want to get some service in,' he said to a pompous, elderly major at Dover who had some complaint about the battalion stores. 'I was running away at Spion Kop when you were still in nappies.' The major gave up.

Kirby was killed by a sniper later that morning. With him at the time was 2/Lt Grayson aged eighteen, who had been at school four months before. Brandon read the burial service over the pair of them, and Brandon, who thought too much, suddenly had a mental picture of a huge map with lines representing men's lives. He saw Grayson's life as a short line from home and school in Hampshire to the Western Front where it stopped. Kirby's began in Halifax, wandered around the globe, India, Ceylon and South Africa, back to England and came to an end in France. Brandon stood thinking after the Last Post and the platoon sergeant thought he had perhaps been a special friend of one of them and was extra upset. However Brandon was not particularly upset; he was intrigued with his idea of the life lines.

But that was looking ahead. Kirby had just moved down the trench when the order came to 'Stand-to' again. These were very good trenches, as some of the men would realize later; they were fairly dry and yet they were deep enough. Some trenches in other areas were too shallow to be much protection and were often half full of water. The regiments in them had used sand-bags to build a parapet in front and a parados behind but they lost a lot of men from snipers and mortar-fire.

2/Lt Brandon now stationed himself ten yards along the trench to the left of Verrall. He was looking at his watch; this was going to be it. Verrall suddenly wanted to sneeze. Plenty of things could happen to your body when you were tensed up and trying not to be scared but this was ridiculous. As he suppressed the sneeze the lieutenant's whistle gave its peculiar throbbing blast. Somehow Verrall was on top of the parapet; the attack had begun.

Verrall always remembered that first time over the top. Later when the experience had been repeated a dozen or more times and in worse circumstances the first still remained printed as vividly as ever on his mind. Surprisingly enough, his first feeling was almost of disappointment. The company jumped over the parapet and began to move forward. It could have been an exercise on Salisbury Plain except that the ground was cut and churned. Any visions he had had of bayoneting huge Germans or dropping on one knee and aiming a swift bullet from his Mark 11 Short Lee-Enfield 303 at a fleeing enemy were instantly dispersed. Any attempts at running would have been a complete fiasco; the ground was so badly cut and holed that maintaining any sort of formation was impossible. All those arrangements for covering fire suddenly seemed quite pointless. It was fortunate that the Germans had stopped shelling altogether. Their lines were only about sixty yards away and not a sign of life was showing in them. Immediately ahead was some damaged barbed wire which would have to be negotiated but that should not be too much trouble. Perhaps the Jerries had fallen back. He skirted round a largish crater. There was some water in the bottom of it and in the water a couple of corpses; they were not British though. Within minutes they were half-way to the German lines and behind he could hear other units following up.

At that moment, when Verrall was half-way across No-Man's-Land, the earth and sky suddenly seemed to explode. With a crash and a thump, splitting your ears and shaking the ground, the guns opened up. My God, he thought, if this was what the Jerries have had to put up with it's no wonder they abandoned their trenches. But these are Jerry shells, he said to himself; they can't be ours firing short. It was an old joke – sort of a joke – in the army that when you didn't know where the shells were coming from they were probably your own. Well, he thought, as blast nearly blew him into a crater, it must be the same with the German gunners.

The air was now dark, gritty, full of fumes and smoke. One great shell, which sent up a huge mountain of earth, managed to spin him round so that he fell down. He climbed to his feet, wondering at first if he had been wounded. Mercifully he had not, but there were screams and shouts around so others had not been so lucky. Curiously enough, although there must have been hundreds of men close to, for the moment he could see nothing; nor did he know which way he was facing. My God, he thought, they've caught us in the open this time. What was happening could not really be true, it must be a dream, or rather a nightmare. He did not even know which direction he was facing. There was now so much smoke drifting over the ground that it was impossible to know where the enemy was or where his own lines were. In the middle of that storm of death he stood there, wondering in which direction he should move.

An ominous sound told him. On his left there suddenly opened up the unmistakable rattle of machine-guns. Obviously someone had got farther than he had. He wondered how. He did not, of course, realize that he had been knocked unconscious by the blast of the last shell and had lain on the ground for a full seven minutes. Suddenly he saw figures around him in the smoke. 'Hi Taffy', he called, 'where the hell are we?' The soldier glanced sideways. It was not Taffy. 'This way lad,' said the man. With a shock Verrall realized he was a stranger, a Scot. Although all rank and regimental badges had been removed before the attack, it was obvious this man belonged to a Scottish regiment. Where had they come from?

The Scot was moving at a steady lope and Verrall found it hard to keep up. It did not matter. Within a few seconds of setting off, he was again lifted right off his feet in a blast which seemed to tear the very ground apart. This time he did not get up so easily. In fact, every time he tried to rise to his feet he fell over again. It took him a minute or two to realize that blood was welling out of a gash in his right knee. That, unfortunately, was not all. The knee joint itself seemed to be broken; every time he tried to put his weight on it to stand up it simply folded up beneath him. Carefully he unwrapped his field dressing and placed it on the wound. Then he realized that part of his trousers was under the dressing; some of the rest was probably in the wound itself. Very carefully and rather slowly, for his movements seemed to have become rather jerky, he cut away the trousers with his jack-knife. The shelling had now quietened down a little but he noted with concern that machine-gun bullets were swishing through the air not far away. He kept well down, then began to crawl along, looking for the nearest shell-hole.

The crater he found was not a new one and it was already

occupied. At the bottom was a small pool of greenish water containing some rags. He did not look too closely at the rags. On the side, facing away from him, was the body of an English soldier. It had taken Verrall a long time to crawl here, the main problem being holding his rifle which kept on catching in the ground. With some misgivings he had shed the trenching tools and his pack. Getting into the shell crater was difficult because if he lost his balance he would pitch down the slope and roll into the water with its vile-looking contents.

Suddenly the 'body' turned; not only was it not dead, it was, Verrall noticed with joy, no other than Taffy Rees. They both exclaimed together, but neither heard a word for another near-by explosion obliterated the sounds. However they were soon talking.

Taffy was not seriously wounded, it seemed. A bullet or perhaps a splinter of shell had gone through his right shoulder completely paralysing his arm. The bleeding had soon stopped. 'I'm what they'd call walking wounded,' he said. 'Except I don't know which way to walk. If I set off and run into Jerry with only my left hand to use he's liable to put his skewer through me a bit quick so I come in here to think it over. It's not much of a wound but I wouldn't mind having a doctor to look at it. I don't seem to be breathing right either.'

Verrall looked at him. Under the dirt Taffy's skin was as white as a sheet. Verrall did not know much about wounds but he suspected this was worse than it looked, but if Taffy was bleeding internally or had had some vital nerves cut there was nothing he could do about it.

They were not by themselves for long. The shelling had not stopped but moved farther away. Verrall felt the ground vibrate. It was funny but he had never thought that anything short of an earthquake could shake the earth. He had soon been proved wrong here.

He felt thirsty and took a swig from his water bottle. He saw Taffy looking at him curiously.

'What's up, Taff?' he said. 'Lost your bottle?'

'Drunk it,' came the reply.

'Drunk it! Blimey, that's a bit quick. You were the one who never drank a drop on a route march.'

'I was thirsty', said Rees, 'but I'm OK.'

'Have a drop of this,' said Verrall. He watched, concerned, at the way Taffy drank, though he did not take much.

The sound of the shelling had now been replaced by an equally ominous sound. At intervals the air above the crater was cut by the sharp, spiteful bite of machine-gun bullets. Following that devastating barrage which had broken up the British attacks the German machine-gunners were keeping the surviving remnants closely pinned down. After a while Verrall and Rees stopped talking; both felt it used up energy they needed, but it was good to have each other there. Then it began to rain. The first few drops came as a surprise and made them both start; somehow it seemed too unfair that in this mess it should start to rain. Both felt bitter at this new affliction. Verrall crawled over to Rees and arranged his groundsheet over him as best he could. Rees had been sitting on it before so now he had the choice of getting soaked or sitting on the cold wet ground. The rain stirred up nauseating smells from the water at the bottom of the crater. Verrall pulled his groundsheet round his shoulders wondering how it was that it had been designed to let the water run into a stream on your calves when you were marching and be too small for anyone but a dwarf to sleep on in comfort. There had been a groundsheet factory in Reading where they'd done some training. All the factory workers got ten times as much pay as a soldier and didn't have to sleep on these rotten groundsheets either. Still, the groundsheets were at least waterproof even if the water did seem to get round and under them.

As they lay miserably huddled in the rain on the wet slopes of the crater another soldier crawled up to the rim and looked over. 'Halt, who goes there? Advance friend and be recognized,' said Taffy, suddenly reviving. The figure pulled himself over and then slid half-way down the greasy slope before he could check his momentum. Then he pulled himself up. He was a stranger, and in pain.

'Who are you?' he asked.

'Who are you?' answered Verrall. He had been warned about Germans infiltrating the lines and obtaining information.

The stranger smiled. 'Fair enough,' he said. 'I'm Captain Driscoll of the 17th Leicesters. Not many of us left I'm afraid. The Germans had a lot of concealed wire, just below a dip in the ground that we couldn't see. They had more machine-guns than we thought. What about you?'

'We're the 1st Edgehills,' said Verrall. 'I just don't know what happened to us. We started off all right but suddenly everything blew apart.'

Driscoll nodded. 'Yes, I know. They outwitted us nicely. They had us taped to a yard from the start. First they put down that box barrage that penned us in just where they wanted, then they let us go forward, then they smashed us up. A bad day, it's been.'

Rees suddenly broke in. 'Will it be in the papers?' he asked.

'Papers', said Driscoll, mystified, 'what papers? Do you mean in your record of service?'

'No, sir,' said Taffy. 'I mean the papers, the newspapers. The *Western Mail*. It's a battle, isn't it? They always report battles.'

Driscoll looked at him sadly. 'It's not a battle,' he said. 'I'm afraid that only the people who were in this lot will know it occurred at all. You'd know what a battle was if you were in one. It would be hundreds of thousands of men, not a few hundred. Sorry. It's bad for us three but it's nothing really.' He looked at Taffy's woebegone expression and wondered whether he should really have told the truth. Still, now it was done.

Verrall looked at him in consternation. 'Do you mean they caught us in a trap?' he asked. 'Guessed what we were doing and so on?'

Driscoll nodded. 'That's about the size of it. God, I wish the bloody rain would stop. Yes, their staff officers must be laughing their heads off. Their intelligence service must be quite bright.'

Verrall stared at him, gradually comprehending. 'You mean they guessed our plans and made them seem easy, then locked us in with that barrage behind us.'

Driscoll nodded and shrugged his shoulders. 'That would be it. They'll put in their counter-attack any time now. This'll be a rough old spot again when they do.

'So they'll come right by here?' said Verrall.

'Probably.'

'What do we do?'

'Well three wounded men can't stop a German battalion. We can try if you like.'

Verrall grinned. It was so long since he had smiled his face felt stiff. 'If they go by here we ought to be able to get one each. They've put us to a lot of trouble these Germans – and not only us . . .' His voice trailed away.

'What do you mean by that?' said Driscoll. 'Of course they have, but who are you thinking of in particular?'

Verrall thought for a moment, then spoke. 'I was thinking of my parents,' he said. 'When I joined up I felt it was a bit rough on them because at times like harvest and winter ploughing you need every pair of hands you can find. I thought it would be all over in six months.'

'Six months!' said Driscoll. 'Good God, it could last six years.'

'Six years!' said Verrall. 'You can't mean it.'

'Well we aren't doing very well at the moment', said Driscoll, 'judging by today. They're using their brains in planning; we're letting all ours be killed as infantry privates. What about yourself? You talk as if you've had an education. Did anyone suggest putting you in for a commission?'

'Yes they did, but I thought the war would be over by the time I got through the extra training. Besides I wanted to know what I'd be like in action before I started leading others. And I got sick of all that bloody rubbish about "officers and gentlemen". Everybody knows that the officers and sergeants have more experience than the privates, but that doesn't mean they should behave like God Almighty. Officers and other ranks! Those who wash and those who have to be made to! Carry on, sarnt-major. That's just what he does. It doesn't happen in civvy street. It's not too bad out here where bullets can't tell the difference, but all that swank and riding breeches on chaps who've never seen a horse and "brother officers", it makes me throw up!' He looked at Driscoll. To his astonishment, Driscoll seemed to have taken nothing in. He might as well have been talking in Eskimo language. 'Well don't you see it, sir?' he said.

Driscoll sighed. 'There it is. France is full of people getting themselves killed as privates in infantry attacks when they ought to be either leading them or being engineers or gunners or at least getting somewhere where they can use their brains and skill. There was a whole battalion I saw once, of chaps who wanted to be with their pals. They called it the public schools battalion. Half of them got wiped out in a show like this.'

He stopped talking. Verrall pulled his rifle close to him and waited for the German counter-attack to begin. But nothing happened. At about 4 p.m. Driscoll said, 'Better give your pal a shake. He ought to try to move a bit. The Germans'll stop playing with these machine-guns after dark and then we might crawl back to our lines. I don't suppose there are enough stretcher-bearers to handle today's casualties.'

Verrall eased closer to Rees and gave him a shake. 'Wake up, Taffy,' he said. 'The officer thinks you ought to take a bit of exercise.' He stopped, and looked more closely. 'Good God, he's dead.' He turned to Driscoll. 'What's happened?' he asked. 'He was all right an hour ago.'

Driscoll shrugged his shoulders. 'Who knows, least of all me. I'm no doctor. The bullet that paralysed his arm probably nicked an artery and he's quietly bled to death – internally of course. It happens.'

'Oh bloody hell,' said Verrall. 'Poor old Taffy. You should have heard him sing. Damned good rugger player too, fly-half, like an eel. Blast these bloody Germans.'

Driscoll looked at him and spoke quietly:

There died a million
And of the best among them
For an old bitch gone in the teeth
For a botched civilization.

Verrall looked at Taffy, at the rain still streaming down, at the sodden figure of what, in better times, was probably a very smart looking captain. 'Do you believe that?' he said.

Driscoll paused. 'Not completely,' he said. 'It was written by an officer I know. He got disillusioned very quickly. I may not have got the words quite right. What he meant, I think, was that the war did not end on the battlefield. We all have to fight on afterwards to build a better world. I'm a regular soldier but I must admit this is a damned silly way of going on and we ought to prevent it. Think of what all this effort could do against poverty and disease. I think that's what he meant.'

'God Almighty,' said Verrall. 'Do you mean to say that when we get out of this stinking lot, if ever we do, we shall have to keep on fighting to prevent it all happening again. By the way, where are you wounded?'

'I'm not quite sure,' said Driscoll. 'I stopped one in the spine. My legs won't work.'

'Let's have a look,' said Verrall. He crawled painfully over. 'My God, you did too. There's a bloody great lump of metal stuck in your backbone. Shall I see if I can pull it out?'

'Great Heavens no. I'll probably bleed to death. Listen, the Germans have stopped traversing their blasted machine-guns and it's just about dark. We ought to get going before they send patrols out. We don't want to be taken prisoner – or bayoneted if they turn nasty.'

Luckily for them, the Germans were satisfied with the day's work and sent out only a few patrols. They already had all the prisoners they needed, captured in the wire in that deceptive little fold in the ground. But it took three and a half hours of painful crawling for Verrall and Driscoll to reach the nearest British trench, where they were nearly shot by a jumpy sentry. Both were given a shot of morphine by an overworked medical officer. Just before Verrall drifted off to sleep he heard the words: 'These two should go to the 3rd Casualty Clearing Station as soon as possible. But they'll have to wait . . . have to wait . . . to wait . . . wait.'

Verrall's wound was more serious than he had thought. After leaving hospital he was sent to an OCTU (Officer Cadet Training Unit) and commissioned into a West Country regiment. Further trouble with his knee caused him to be posted to the Depot rather than France and he found the experience boring and frustrating. He volunteered for the Royal Flying Corps and also the Royal Tank Corps but his commanding officer told the adjutant to lose his applications for, he said, 'When I get a decent instructor I'm not going to have him wandering off to be a bloody birdman or shut himself up in a tin like a sardine. He'll stay with the regiment where he can be useful.'

When Verrall finally went abroad again it turned out to be Palestine. For one month, after heavy casualties, he commanded the battalion, showing considerable verve and dash but then – to everyone's disgust – he was replaced by an elderly lieutenant-colonel who appeared to have been resurrected for the purpose. All his war so far had been spent in administrative jobs, and his arrival was bitterly resented by all the officers except, curiously enough, Verrall. For his part, the new CO was firmly convinced that anyone who was not a Regular could not possibly understand soldiering, no matter what his experience. He had played cricket for Harrow against Eton twenty years before and would frequently give a ball by ball account of this and other matches to junior officers bored to the limit of endurance. Apart from this he was kind, fussily competent, and as completely indifferent to shellfire as he was to other people's opinions.

Verrall's own insignificance in the military hierarchy was clearly set out in official War Office communications which referred to him as Lt, Acting Captain, Temporary Major Verrall. He was in fact mentioned twice in despatches but did not discover the fact till long afterwards, as they were usually on the move. His demobilization was delayed 'owing to the exigencies of the services' and it was late 1919 before he was back in Oxfordshire as a civilian. People said 'You've changed.' He thought they had changed too but not for the better, but he had learned to keep his opinions to himself. He married in 1921 and his daughter was born in early 1922. When she was eighteen she met a young American whose father used to make periodic visits to an agricultural machinery subsidiary company at Banbury. His name was Steve Varley, and they still wrote to each other after he had returned to Nebraska.

VARLEY

The American Soldier of the Second World War

'The Japanese', the major had said, 'do not think in the way that we Americans do. The individual counts for nothing and they will continue fighting long after there has ceased to be any point in doing so.'

There had been that and a lot more. They'd listened to talks on Shintoism and the Samurai, on Japanese habits, and Japanese weapons, they'd seen films taken early in the war, and they'd been told over and over again about Jap fanaticism. It was typical of the way the army went on. They didn't seem to think that by harping on about what marvellous fighters the Japs were they might be scaring the pants off a lot of people. It was only when you saw our aeroplanes and guns and ships you realized the Japs couldn't win. There was a wisecrack going around about a Jap prisoner being interrogated.

'Who are the best jungle fighters?' they'd asked.

'The Australians, I think,' he said.

'And the second best?'

'The British.'

'What about the Americans?'

'Oh I don't know about that. They've usually blown it away with their bombs and guns and us with it.'

A typical bit of lying propaganda. You could pound these slant-eyed yellow bastards with H.E. until the ground looked as if it had been bulldozed, but as soon as you set foot on it the Japs would spring up out of their holes, lobbing grenades, and yelling *Banzai*. I bet that major who gave us all those lectures – and all his pals – had never seen a Jap outside California. And as for jungle, they wouldn't know what the word meant.

Varley wiped his forehead and stared down the track. It seemed a bit unlikely the Japs would walk right into the ambush as easily as all that, but you never could tell.

Last week a guy in B company, who'd been in New Guinea, said that once when they were watching a road a whole company of Japs rode down it on bicycles. On bicycles! They killed half of them. There was no doubt the Japs were crazy and not only on religion and the Emperor and all that lot. Someone said they actually tried to get killed because that way they went straight to heaven.

Well if one showed upon this path he'd go fast. He'd get the whole clip. Varley was fed up with the Japs. He hadn't volunteered off the farm in order to fight in this stinking jungle, but like a fool he had rushed off to volunteer. Why?

Why? What a damfool question. Because of a dame of course. Why did anyone volunteer. He volunteers to impress some dame, or maybe he thinks he'll do a bit better with the dames when he's inside a uniform.

A leech dropped off the branch above him and began questing along his arm. He brushed it off quickly before it got its teeth in.

Well he'd volunteered because of a dame too. What a sucker! She was a great kid and he'd met her in the fall of 1938 when they were visiting Banbury, England. They were both kids but it looked like the real thing. After Pearl Harbor he'd joined the army thinking he'd get sent to Europe and stationed in England. Nobody thought of there being much army in the Pacific; everyone was saying we'd do for the Japs by aircraft carriers and subs. It was a great thought. He couldn't help smiling a bit even in this sweaty stinking spot.

Still, it could be worse. He had a nice little combat job, well away from headquarters and all that crap. He was in 69 Group. You might think there were sixty-eight other groups but you'd be wrong. 69 was just a handy number (it read the same upside down) for an outfit like theirs. There were eighty-two of them; there used to be 120 and all the casualties had been from disease. That was the real enemy out here, not the Japs, although the Japs made a good second. The group's job was to lose themselves in the jungle here, in the Solomons, and harry the Japs. It sounded difficult but it was not too bad. Everything was so much bigger than it looked on a map. They put two or three dots on a map but when you got there you found there were about a couple of hundred little islands, mostly uninhabited. Sometimes the Japs cottoned on to where they were and sent out a patrol or something to finish them off. They had no idea these Japs; 69 Group would lead the patrol on and – whoosh – that would be a few more Japs for nirvana.

He reckoned he was lucky to be with this outfit although there were doubtless plenty who would not have the job for anything in the world. Six months before, just after they'd arrived in the Pacific theatre, a signal had gone to all units asking for volunteers for a special mission. The volunteers would need to be young, fit, good shots, resourceful, experienced sailors, and so on. Some people in the army volunteer for nothing, others volunteer for everything; either way you're in trouble. If you volunteer you might find yourself posted to some lousy unit that consists of all the deadbeats and throwouts that any real regiment wouldn't have or you might find yourself on a crackerjack mission with the best guys in the world. The guys who never volunteer but hope to save their skins usually get the worst of it; they get turned into experimental glider regiments or something and become part of the statistics which make HQ decide the experiment is too costly. You can't beat the system in the army.

The real snag with this job was what he was doing now, sitting around waiting for something to happen. Meanwhile the mosquitoes ate you, the monkeys laughed at you and you got skin rash from sweating too long without changing your position. And you were stuck with your own thoughts. You would take up position soon after dawn and stay still – or nearly still – for hour after hour. The only thing you could do was think. It was all right for the guys with pleasant memories and hopes for a future after the war, but for the lost guys it was plain murder. Poor old Luigi. Some kind neighbour had sent him a letter last week saying his wife was going out with a marine and neglecting the kids. Of course, Luigi doted on the kids; he didn't care too much about his wife. There was nothing, but nothing, that Luigi could do but sit and sweat it out, but it didn't make him a better soldier. It was rough on the married guys. Not that they acted like saints – who would out here – but they'd got all their eggs in one basket. 'Dear Jim, the automobile broke down yesterday but I got a lift from Cary Spatz. He's a real nice guy and you'd like him. He's offered to help mend that broken window in my bedroom I told you about . . .' Jim had let off his carbine by accident and ruined the ambush last Monday. Maybe he thought it was the 'real nice guy' coming into his sights! He's too jumpy altogether. He ought to be evacuated. Guys like that are a problem.

Varley glanced at his watch. Eleven o'clock. Were the little bastards coming or weren't they? Come on you little monkey men, these bloody insects will have eaten all the skin off my bones.

Yes, that was it. They'd called for volunteers and he'd offered. It was all a great mystery. Could you swim, could you climb mountains, could you cook! When they asked if he had done much sailing he said 6,000 miles. They were impressed. They did not ask him for details which was just as well because explaining that the 6,000 miles had been there and back across the Atlantic in a liner which was so big you forgot you were at sea – well that would have been embarrassing. He'd soon learnt to handle the boats they used out here.

Speaking frankly he could not see how squatting here on a jungle path waiting for a tattered Jap to push his little peaked cap round the corner was really going to win the war. Those beach landings – he'd been in one – were really something. Waiting bunched up in a transport you felt like a single component in a General Motors car-assembly line. First the aircraft went over, hundreds of them pounding all the beachheads and Jap forts, then the navy had a go. You wouldn't believe there could be so many ships anywhere, the sea was just covered with them. When they opened up they certainly made one hell of a noise at this end so God knows what it was like at the other. In fact his own battalion hadn't been needed – they were only in reserve anyway. But when they had gone ashore it had been an eye-opener. There were bodies all over the place, and not only Japs, our boys too, hundreds of them. Whether those guns and bombs had all been on the wrong target couldn't be known but there were certainly plenty of live Japs waiting to receive. One of the guys rolled over a Jap and tried to pull out his teeth. The sergeant had made him stop it but the guy had gone on grumbling all day about the fact that the marines were making a fortune out of the gold teeth they pulled out of Jap corpses. Out here the Japs (and Chinese too) put their savings on their teeth in the shape of gold. Me, I'd rather be poor than make money pulling Jap teeth. I don't believe the marines would do it either, even if they had time. It's the details who follow, grave-digger parties and that lot. Someone sent his wife a paper knife made out of a Jap thigh-bone. There was a row in the States over that, the bible-punchers didn't like it. Out here things look different. When you first see a bunch of bones you shudder and feel glad it's not you. After a few hundred you don't even think about it at all.

Ten minutes later Captain Gilson came up the path behind and gave the order to stand down. If the Japs had not come by now, they wouldn't be coming today. The Japs were marvellous fighters but they were fortunately a bit predictable.

In an hour's time the Japs would be having *mishi*; that was their midday meal. They could go for days on a bit of dried fish and hope, but when they got a chance they settled down to a meal of cooked rice and savoury soup.

There were sixteen members of Group 69 in this ambush party today and, having posted sentries, the captain briefed the remainder. 'They've given up trying to find us,' he said. 'We'll go and find them. We'll give them some digestion pills.'

Gilson was like that; he thought he was a great comedian. Some of the boys didn't understand half of what he was on about. He was a bit kooky, was Gilson, but he knew his job. 'We'll go and shoot up their chow line', he said. 'An Aussie I met in Port Moresby told me they've got detachments in the jungle doing just the same as we are. The Limeys are doing it in Burma too. This Aussie said they got a lot of their kills when the Nips* were at the rice buckets. If that lot has been looking for us all morning they'll be back in camp any moment and very hungry. They won't expect to find us there. But we need to move fast.'

'Moving fast' in the jungle is, of course, a ludicrous exaggeration. If the vegetation is fairly light and there are tracks made by animals or natives who have discreetly vanished; if you know the way, you can move, all being well, about two miles an hour. But if you have to penetrate thick jungle or swamp you can spend all day getting hardly anywhere at all. Fortunately much of their present terrain was in the former category, but like all the jungle it was not to be trusted. You might decide to sit on the trunk of a fallen tree only to discover it crumbled with dust and sent you sprawling among a nest of scorpions or you might come across an attractive little pool, with clear water and a sandy bottom; not until four days later would you learn you were dying of leptospirosis.

All this was known, and only the careless or stupid made mistakes. What no one could control were the insects and mysterious fevers. The soldiers were all bunged full of prophylactics against the known hazards like malaria and dengue (sometimes they even said they'd rather have the fever than the prophylactic), but there was always the unknown ague which the medics didn't seem to know about. After all, why should they. No one had ever been in this God-forsaken hole before and if they were in their right minds no one would ever want to go here again after the war; he certainly wouldn't himself.

After three-quarters of an hour's sweating and stumbling Gilson put them on to 'stalking drill'. This manoeuvre belonged to no known military tactic but was a peculiar approach method developed by guerrilla groups like themselves. No one moves silently in the jungle, it is not possible; there is always a rotten stick which crunches underfoot or a startled bird. There is plenty of noise anyway in the jungle, cicadas, birds, monkeys

*Short for Nipponese. Nippon – Japan.

and other contributors, mostly very small; even so, it doesn't
do to sound like an elephant because that will quieten the
other noises. Practice had made 69 Group adept at making no
more noise than the rest of the average-sized denizens. As they
came closer Varley felt a strange drumming excitement. He was
still thinking, of course. It's odd, he thought, that a hundred-
per-cent American like me should be getting such a kick out of
this sort of task. It seems quite natural too. That's very curious.
Why should a farmer like me get into this sort of outfit at all?
(Possibly Vaylo or Varelle, or Rolf or Tolosa could have told
him, as could any of the others whose blood in smaller or
greater quantity ran through his veins; perhaps, from their own
particular nirvanas they were watching his progress. Pietro
would certainly have been interested to see the developments
made in 'fire gonnes' and Varrus would have been intrigued to
see the use he made of cover).

As they formed a line along the inside of the jungle fringe the
sight that met their eyes was most encouraging. The Japanese
had built themselves two long *attap* huts in a clearing (attap
was a long flat leaf which thatched the roof and covered the
sides of these bamboo structures). Outside was a smaller hut
which was presumably used as a ration store, and on the other
side was a square building with a little attap fence round it.
That looked like the accommodation of an officer, or perhaps a
warrant-officer. On the far side of the clearing there were three
other long huts but these were still being constructed. Clearly
this detachment had the task of building camps for the arrival
of reinforcements. That was interesting. Where did the Japs
think they were heading for?

Over a trench fire in front of the huts there was a whole row
of small dixies; to the left were two large, flat pans of the type
that were known out here as quarleys; these were steaming.
One would be full of rice, the other of stew. The Japs were all
inside the huts, probably lying down, resting after their exer-
tions in the heat. A few minutes later the Japanese cook, a
stumpy little man with a very flat head, who was wearing

nothing but a 'G-string', stood up and made a peculiar cry. It did not sound much like human speech but it was understood all right. Out of the hut came the Japs, each carrying his little dixie, and dressed only in his G-string. The G-string covers even less than a bikini. The sight gave 69 Group infinite pleasure, not because it was a joy to look on near nude Japanese but because not a single one was carrying a weapon. Chattering happily with strange hissing speech they lined up expectantly. As the first one was receiving his dollop of rice, Gilson gave the order.

What followed seemed almost impossible to believe. As the bullets from the automatics cut into the line of Japanese they fell like grass before a scythe. Gilson took no part in this; he had raced across the clearing to the officer's hut. The occupant had not appeared, doubtless he was waiting for an orderly to bring his rice to the hut. Instead the figure who appeared in the entrance was Gilson, who held the track record for the 100 at Yale but who had never run as fast as he did today – ever. The Japanese officer might or might not be stripped off like the men. Whether or not, he would have a weapon near by, probably an automatic. A lot of these Japs out here had poor quality rifles and relied mainly on mortars and grenades. They were very handy indeed with their mortars and could drop the bomb on a target with amazing accuracy. However, they had captured a lot of Thompson sub-machine guns in the Philippines and elsewhere and automatics were more plentiful.

Whatever weapon the Japanese officer had he was given no opportunity to use it. Gilson lobbed a grenade through the open door and ran on. Just before the grenade exploded he flung himself on to the ground. The attap house disintegrated with the dull toneless thump of the grenade; Gilson had twisted over and was pointing his revolver at the ruins in case anything living should emerge. Nothing did but the hut was soon crackling away merrily sending a long column of black smoke into the sky. Gilson strolled over to the group, still holding his revolver and looking very much alert. 'Goddamn,' he said, 'the other

Japs will know they've had visitors. They won't find us but they could be a nuisance. Collect any papers you can find, and anything useful to intelligence. Don't waste your time on souvenirs. You're soldiers, not antique collectors. Get looking.'

'What about their weapons?' asked one of the soldiers. 'Pile them up here with the ammo,' said Gilson. 'We'd better not chuck them on to the fire. We'll lay a little trail so that this heap will burn after we've gone. Bring some attap.'

'That'll do it,' said Gilson after a few minutes. 'Now scram. Once that lot lights up there'll be bullets spitting in all directions.'

Back in the jungle it seemed cooler, though oppressive. They stopped for a short break and ate. Gilson looked impatient. 'It doesn't smell right to me,' he said. 'There are a lot of Japs knocking round on this end of the island and I have a feeling they might be looking for us. This goddam area smells bad to me.'

In mid-afternoon it was so hot that a storm seemed inevitable. Gilson took them through one edge of a mangrove swamp. 'I've got a feeling about that track we've been following,' he said. 'We wouldn't want to meet strangers with us not being in our best clothes, would we?'

Nobody smiled, but they appreciated the attempt at a joke none the less. The track they were on wound gently upwards. It led, after a while, to their base, where on a ridge they had good observation and several points of quick retreat.

Half a mile along this track it happened. It was so incongruous they could hardly believe it. Being so near base the group had relaxed and were plodding along wearily, Indian fashion, looking forward to a well-earned rest. Suddenly, round the corner, came a Japanese patrol, rifles slung, laughing and talking. Afterwards the American discovered they had been visiting a native village. Visiting meant raping the women and drinking the local *sake* wine; they too felt they had done a good day's work.

The two groups were in such close contact at once that it was impossible to fire or use a grenade for fear of doing as much damage to your own side as to the enemy. The only weapon was bayonet or knife. And there in the heart of the Pacific, representatives of two highly-equipped modern armies fought each other hand-to-hand like tribes before guns were invented. It was fortunate the Japanese were drunk and a pity they were not slightly drunker. By the time the fight was over ten minutes later seven Americans were dead and all twelve Japanese. Nobody looked a very pleasant sight. Gilson, who looked as if he had been helping in a butcher's shop, lit a cigarette and offered one to Varley. 'Well done, man,' he said. 'You and I were born in the wrong age. I enjoyed that. I reckon you and I would have made a good go of things in the Stone Age.'

Varley grinned. 'Maybe we did,' he said.

'Oh, I don't go in for that reincarnation crap', answered Gilson, 'but man if I'd seen you moving around like you did a few minutes ago I'd certainly have made you a chief.'

Varley smiled wearily. 'Thanks, Captain. I think I'll settle for my present job though.'

'Me too,' said Gilson. 'There's only one good thing about the past. It can never come back, and neither you nor I, Varley, are going to be a mite different for what happened hundreds of years ago. Now let's get on with winning this goddamn war.'